Richard Webster was born in 1950. He studied English Literature at the University of East Anglia, where he has also taught. His articles have appeared in *Critical Quarterly, Quarto, The Literary Review, The Observer* and *The Bookseller*. He is working on a study of the relationship between ancient religions and modern political totalitarianism.

In 1985 he and his wife started The Orwell Bookshop in Southwold.

A Brief History of
BLASPHEMY

Liberalism, Censorship and
'The Satanic Verses'

RICHARD WEBSTER

The Orwell Press

First published in Great Britain in 1990 by
The Orwell Press
64 High Street
Southwold
Suffolk IP18 6DN

ISBN 0 9515922 0 3

Phototypeset by Saxon Printing Ltd, Derby
Printed and bound by Cox & Wyman Ltd, Reading

Acknowledgments

Grateful acknowledgment is made to *The Observer* for permission to reprint a substantial part of Julie Flint's article, 'Tragedy in the name of Allah', which appeared in the paper on February 11th 1990.

The two black and white drawings incorporated into the design of this book are by Chris Evans and are taken from Karen Armstrong's *Holy War*, Macmillan, 1988. At the time of going to press it had not been possible to identify the owner of the copyright.

Contents

Preface

This book began life as a pamphlet – a piece of *samizdat* literature produced on a photocopier and circulated privately to a small number of writers, journalists and historians during the last week of January 1990.

The pamphlet consisted of the first two chapters of the present book. I wrote it because, having some familiarity with the history of blasphemy and of the role which it has played in religious persecution, I felt that I had something to say about the *Satanic Verses* affair which might be of interest.

Perhaps more importantly still, I was disturbed by the course that the debate had taken and alarmed at how little analysis there had been of the underlying issues.

My pamphlet came too late to have any effect on the debate during the period leading up to the first anniversary of the *fatwa*. But it did elicit a warm and enthusiastic response in a number of quarters, some of them unexpected. Subsequently several people urged me to make what I had written more widely available.

This book is the result.

Because the debate has moved on so rapidly in the months since my pamphlet was written, I have added three new chapters to the original two. In these I have included a reply to Salman Rushdie's essay 'In Good Faith'. I have also given an account of some of the more recent stages of the debate.

The two parts of the book reflect the different circumstances in which they were written. The first part is more reflective and historical. The second part is more down-to-earth, more clearly focused on the details of the recent debate, and on some of the real consequences of the *Satanic Verses* affair in Bradford and elsewhere. I hope that the two parts of the book will complement one another.

They are linked by a section which reproduces a number of Christian woodcuts and engravings, most of which were included in my original pamphlet. There is sometimes a tendency on the part of readers to disregard illustrations or to treat them rather less seriously than the text in which they appear. For in our puritanical culture we are taught from an early age to overcome our predilection for pictures and to cultivate a more serious interest in the word. This attitude goes deep into our history; in particular our Puritan contempt for religious images can be found scored into the fabric of nearly every ancient church in Britain, just as it is stamped bleakly on the bare walls of every non-conformist chapel.

Yet our religious tradition was preserved and disseminated by images for many centuries. Literacy is a latecomer to history and if we disregard the image we are in danger of disregarding the human imagination itself. It is because, ultimately, this book is about the human imagination, and the power of the imagination, that it contains images as well as words. The illustrations, including the manuscript illustration which is reproduced on the front cover, are not offered merely as adornments or diversions. For they, and the commentaries on them, are an integral part of the argument.

Because it seemed necessary to produce this book at breakneck speed, it has not proved possible to incorporate the normal apparatus of footnotes and an index. I have included a bibliography, however, and in nearly all cases it should be possible to identify the source of quotations by reference to it.

Entries in the bibliography are for the most part self-explanatory. I would like to draw attention, however, to the three booklets produced by the Commission for Racial Equality in conjunction with the Policy Studies Unit, the Runnymede Trust and the Inter Faith Network. These booklets take the form of reports on seminars organised by the Commission during 1989. This description, however, and their rather dull and official-looking covers, belies their fascinating content. They are immensely valuable and should be more widely known than they are.

While I have been writing this book many people have given generously of their time in order to answer my queries or read drafts. I am grateful to them all.

In the final stages of preparing my manuscript for publication I received a great deal of help from two friends, Ruth Whittaker and

Derek Hall. I am particularly grateful to them for their constructive suggestions and for their help and support. The same is true of Hugh Forbes who, even though we have never met, gave up his time generously and unstintingly to make this a better book than it would otherwise have been. I cannot thank him enough.

Finally I want to thank my wife. Without her encouragement and her help this book could not and would not have been written.

Southwold, April 1990

Introduction

One of the most important questions posed by the *Satanic Verses* affair is whether a particular freedom which British citizens now possess to a limited degree – the freedom to blaspheme against their neighbours' religion – is a precious freedom which should be defended at all costs. If it is indeed a precious freedom, then not only should *The Satanic Verses* immediately be published in paperback, but our current blasphemy laws should be abolished. For at the moment we are *not* free to blaspheme against our neighbours' religion if they happen to be Christians.

Throughout the debate which was started by the publication of *The Satanic Verses* a number of influential novelists, writers and journalists have campaigned for both these objectives. Many of them have done so under the aegis of the International Committee for the Defence of Salman Rushdie and his Publishers, a committee which was originally created by the free speech organisation, Article 19.

In order to further its campaign the International Committee has produced a pamphlet under the title *The Crime of Blasphemy – Why It Should Be Abolished*. Copies of this pamphlet have been widely distributed to members of the International Committee's constituent organisations, including all members of the Publishers' Association; copies have also been sent to MPs and to the Home Office. The pamphlet is well produced and energetically argued. Its contention that the current blasphemy laws are in need of reform seems an eminently just one. For, as its authors observe:

> The Muslim community in Britain has thought to invoke the laws on blasphemy in their campaign to suppress *The Satanic Verses*. Distress over the novel can only have been increased with the discovery that the existing law protects Christianity alone and not other faiths such as Islam. Such discrimination in the law is unacceptable...

The most controversial element in the International Committee's pamphlet, however, is not the proposal that the current blasphemy laws should be abolished, but the confident recommendation that they should be abolished *without replacement*. For the argument which is put forward to justify this view raises immense difficulties. In what follows I have not attempted to counter the International Committee's suggestions by framing alternative proposals for reforming the law. What I have tried to do is to show that the whole subject of blasphemy is more complex and more fraught with real contemporary dangers than the International Committee itself ever allows.

I have called my book 'A Brief History of Blasphemy' after the fourth and final section of the International Committee's own document. The first chapter of the book might also be called 'An Alternative History of Blasphemy'. For it is an attempt to show, without ever aspiring to completeness or comprehensiveness, that the picture of blasphemy which is presented by the authors of the International Committee's document is incomplete, and in some respects, seriously misleading. The real history of blasphemy, and of the role it has played in religious and secular conflicts, is a great deal more complex and a great deal more disturbing.

One of my reservations about the view of blasphemy which is advanced in the Committee's pamphlet is that it seems to be based on an orthodox approach to history, and above all on the unconscious adoption of a Christian perspective. To those most closely involved with writing the pamphlet, I suspect that this will seem a strange, if not an extraordinary claim. For the dominant tone is certainly not a Christian one and derives rather from the secularist and humanist traditions. But I am talking about a cultural attitude rather than a theological one. The problem is simply that in Western Europe over the course of at least ten centuries an exclusively Christian perspective on history has become so powerful, and has been so deeply internalised into our culture that it has become an almost invisible habit of mind. More than ten years ago Michael Dummett, in his introduction to R.C. Zaehner's *The City Within the Heart*, argued that it is a bad habit. Having discussed the common cultural heritage which Muslim and Christian culture share, including their common roots in the Jewish religious tradition, he wrote that 'It is senseless to treat the history of Christendom as a unit: the history of Christians, Jews and Muslims can only be dealt with as a whole'.

This view has not generally found favour among historians. But there is one very significant exception. In her book, *Holy War*, which is a profound study of the religious origins of the modern Middle East conflict, Karen Armstrong arrives independently at the same conclusion, and states it with some vehemence:

> I am vehement because since my first visits to Israel in 1983 I have come to feel very passionate about the relationship between the Christian West and Judaism and Islam, which have been locked in a murderous triangle of hatred ever since the Crusades.
>
> What I am arguing for is a triple vision. Usually when we strive to be objective we say that we want to see 'both' sides of the question. In this long conflict, however, there are three. At each point I shall try to consider the position and point of view of Jews, Christians and Muslims – the three religions of Abraham. Since the Crusades all three have been implicated in different ways in the holy wars between them. The greatest tragedies and atrocities have occurred when one tradition considers itself so pre-eminent that it seeks to eliminate the other two, or when two of the traditions have joined forces, and have completely ignored the third.

I am indebted to Karen Armstrong's book and grateful for her large vision. What I have tried to show in the pages which follow is that what she calls 'triple vision' is just as necessary to an understanding of the history of blasphemy as it is to the understanding of any other aspect of our history.

But I must also record another debt. For ever since, as an undergraduate supposed to be studying literature, I stumbled upon the work of Norman Cohn, I have been influenced by his approach to history.

In three widely acclaimed books, *The Pursuit of the Millennium*, *Warrant for Genocide*, and *Europe's Inner Demons*, Professor Cohn has explored one of the most enduring of the irrational impulses which lie behind Judaeo-Christian history – 'the urge to purify the world through the annihilation of some category of human beings imagined as agents of corruption and incarnations of evil'. In doing so he has thrown more light on the history and dynamics of persecution and prejudice than perhaps any other living British historian.

Though the position which I now occupy is somewhat different from his, the example of Professor Cohn's work and of his rich historical imagination has always been, and will always remain, an inspiration.

Part One

CHAPTER ONE

A Brief History of Blasphemy

On February 14th 1989 the Ayatollah Khomeini pronounced his *fatwa*, which was in effect a death threat against Salman Rushdie and his publishers. Since then *The Satanic Verses* has probably occasioned more comment in newspapers and journals than any book ever published, including *Lady Chatterley's Lover*. The reaction to the novel has been the subject of at least five conferences and five books in the United Kingdom alone. In view of this it might well seem that everything that can be said about the *Satanic Verses* affair has been said. I believe, however, that some of the underlying issues have scarcely been dealt with at all, and that there are a number of fundamental questions which still need to be both asked and answered.

In order to avoid any misunderstanding I should start by making it clear that I am in no doubt at all that the Ayatollah Khomeini's reaction to *The Satanic Verses* was cruel and tyrannical, and that one of its main purposes was to shore up the narrow and repressive regime which he had established in Iran. Armed censorship of this kind is totally unacceptable. For the sake of Salman Rushdie himself and for the sake of his publishers, no effort should be spared to bring about the lifting of the death threat.

To say this, however, is by no means to concur with all the opinions which have been expressed by those who, with every justification, have offered Salman Rushdie their support. Indeed, I am bound to confess that ever since the Rushdie affair started there is one thing I have feared more than the bombs of Islamic fundamentalists. It is the harm that can be done by the machine-gun bullets of liberal self-righteousness. The ricochet of those bullets can be heard all too clearly in the chauvinistic tones of Fay Weldon's Counterblast pamphlet, *Sacred Cows*, and in the hard rhetoric of those who have been demanding the immediate publication of *The Satanic Verses* in paperback. If we allow ourselves to be swayed by such rhetoric we are in danger, I believe, of seeing with disproportionate clarity the cruelty and repressiveness of Islam, while failing to register at all the rigidity and authoritarianism of some of our own most precious cultural traditions.

What we need is a little less pressure on the trigger of cultural patriotism, and a little more historical perspective. For only then is it likely that we can take a more balanced and considered view of the particular dilemma which still faces Penguin Books and of the more general dilemma which is going to face Western writers and intellectuals for many years to come, whether they like it or not.

Of all the issues which are raised by the *Satanic Verses* affair, and which clamour for discussion, blasphemy is both one of the most important and one of the most difficult. It is difficult, partly because in our own society the law against blasphemy is widely regarded as an archaic one – a kind of legal appendix, which still survives in the body politic, but which seems to have no real function.

The last time a case of blasphemy was brought before the courts was in 1977, when Mary Whitehouse instituted a private prosecution against *Gay News* for publishing a poem by James Kirkup which seemingly portrayed Jesus as the object of homosexual love. Although this prosecution was successful, one of the effects of Mary Whitehouse's action was to bring the laws of blasphemy, which had not been invoked for more than half a century, into active disrepute, particularly among writers and poets. In the same year that the prosecution was brought against *Gay News*, a number of humanist organisations founded the Committee Against Blasphemy Law and carried forward a vigorous campaign to abolish the offence. Although this campaign attracted considerable support, it bore no immediate fruit in spite of the fact that the abolition of the offence of blasphemy was also advocated in 1979 by the Bernard Williams Committee in its *Report on Obscenity and Film Censorship*.

The cause of the abolitionists attracted even more support in 1985 when the Law Commission published its report, *Criminal Law: Offences against Religion and Public Worship*, which, broadly speaking, endorsed the humanist view. It described the common law offences of blasphemy and blasphemous libel as 'unsatisfactory and archaic'. It noted that the law offered protection against blasphemy only to Christianity and went on to argue that in the multi-cultural United

Kingdom of the late twentieth century this 'could not be justified'. The Law Commissioners were not, as we will eventually see, unanimous in their conclusion. But it is clearly significant that their main report concluded by recommending abolition of the common law offence 'without replacement'.

In 1989, when Muslims in Britain sought unsuccessfully to invoke the blasphemy laws against Penguin Books for publishing *The Satanic Verses*, the humanist and libertarian campaigns against the blasphemy laws were revived. In particular, Article 19, a free speech pressure group based in London, took the initiative in forming an International Committee for the Defence of Salman Rushdie and his Publishers. As well as organising support for the threatened author, this committee began to campaign against the blasphemy laws. Meanwhile, in Parliament on 12th April 1989, Tony Benn presented a bill to the House of Commons to abolish the offence of blasphemy. He was supported by MPs from all parties including David Steel and Sir Ian Gilmour. Soon after this the International Committee published its pamphlet *The Crime of Blasphemy – Why it Should be Abolished*.

This pamphlet is, in some respects, a valuable one – not least because it is informed, like most humanist or secularist arguments, by a strong sense of history. One of the ideas which has grown up around the blasphemy laws is that their main purpose is to protect the tender sensitivities of Christians. It is certainly true that the laws against blasphemy have often served to do just this. But the International Committee puts forward a much more robust view of their traditional function. This view is perhaps most forcefully expressed in a passage it quotes from an earlier pamphlet, Chapman Cohen's *Blasphemy – a Plea for Religious Equality*, which was published in 1922:

> Blasphemy laws are a heritage from a wicked and deplorable past. In their essence they belong to a period when laws were far more ferocious than they are today, and when it was held the duty of the State to enforce and openly coerce opinion. They are also part of the general belief that the right discharge of the duties of citizenship depends, in some more or less obscure way, on the holding of right religious beliefs. In such circumstances, unbelief, heresy and blasphemy partake of the nature of treason. The heretic is one who is a threat to the welfare of the tribe or nation, and, in the interests of the whole group, he must be suppressed...

> The blasphemy laws are aimed at opinion and opinion alone. It is
> to the spirit of persecution they owe their existence; it is the spirit
> of intolerance and persecution they always serve.

This passage could scarcely be described as embodying a
dispassionate approach to history. But it is precisely because of this
that it manages to convey a much more accurate picture of the role
played in our own history by religious repression than will be found
in the work of most academic historians. That Cohen's view is not
only robust, but also realistic, is amply attested by the way in which
the crime of blasphemy was tried over a period of at least three
centuries.

The current British law on blasphemy developed during the
seventeenth century. It grew out of the much older law of heresy
which was designed to protect the Christian church against all
forms of dissidence. Until the end of the nineteenth century this
law was frequently invoked with a quite vicious repressiveness
against those who made disrespectful references to God or Jesus or
the Church. In particular, ribaldry or obscenity directed against
Christianity was rigorously outlawed. Even those who rebelled on
doctrinal matters or who questioned the doctrine of the eternal
punishment of the wicked might find themselves arraigned on a
charge of blasphemy and they could by no means be certain of
acquittal. In 1729, for example, the Cambridge academic and deist,
Thomas Woolston, was successfully prosecuted for writing a series
of pamphlets in which he anticipated the present Bishop of Durham
by denying the literal truth of the miracles of the New Testament
and arguing that they should be construed allegorically. These
pamphlets were held to have struck 'at the very root of Christianity'
and Woolston was detained until he died in 1733.

Woolston's fate was relatively mild. For originally, at least, the
punishment of blasphemers sometimes involved not only
imprisonment but also torture. In 1656, for example, James Nayler,
a Quaker from Bristol, was charged with claiming equality with
God. He was tried before the High Court of Parliament, and it was
decreed 'that he be repeatedly set in the pillory and scourged; that
he be branded on the forehead with the letter 'B'; that he have his
tongue bored with a red hot iron and be confined afterwards in
prison and set to hard labour'.

In 1676, during the trial of an apparently deranged man, who
claimed that Jesus Christ was a bastard and a whore-master and

that religion was a cheat, the Lord Chief Justice, Sir Matthew Hale, first laid down the principle that Christianity was part of the law of England, and that a threat to the Church was, by its very nature, a threat to the State. He said: 'That such kind of wicked and blasphemous words were not only an offence against God and religion but a crime against the laws, States and Government...and therefore punishable in this court, that to say religion is a cheat, is to dissolve all those obligations whereby civil societies are preserved; and Christianity being parcel of the laws of England, therefore to reproach Christian religion is to speak in subversion of the law.'

Hale's judgment, which was to influence British law for centuries, sprang from what might be termed 'the floodgate theory' of morality. This theory almost always operates in nascent or immature democracies. In such democracies laws against freedom of expression are invoked frequently and censorship is often pervasive and violently enforced. We can see this clearly in the history of attitudes towards obscenity. For in this country as in others the responsibility and restraint which were considered a precondition of the 'freedom of expression' which we now enjoy were inculcated into successive generations through a long series of purity campaigns. The organisers of these campaigns never hesitated to use the most violent sanctions provided by the law, in order to restrain the sexual imagination and outlaw any form of art which might be deemed immoral.

Again and again campaigners for purity have invoked the 'floodgate theory'; they have warned that to relax the rigour of the law in the smallest way, to allow even a trickle of transgression, will ultimately lead to a flood of immorality which it will be beyond the power of governments to control.

Those who have campaigned with the most vigilance against blasphemy have frequently done so for similar reasons, often invoking the 'floodgate theory' directly by arguing that, if blasphemy were to be tolerated in a single instance, impiety might rapidly spread throughout the land. Indeed, there has always been a close relationship between obscenity laws and blasphemy laws, with obscene or scurrilous language tending to be construed as one of the characteristics of blasphemy. In an important judgment delivered in 1883 Lord Chief Justice Coleridge incorporated this view into what was, in effect, a redefinition of the law. 'If the

decencies of controversy are observed,' he maintained, 'even the
fundamentals of religion may be attacked without a person being
guilty of blasphemous libel.' The same view of the law was upheld
in 1917 during the case of *Bowman v Secular Society Ltd*. In this case
it was maintained that a company which had been formed to
promote the secularisation of society was not unlawful even though
one of its objects was to deny Christianity. Blasphemous words are
punishable 'for their manner, their violence, or ribaldry, or, more
fully stated, for their tendency to endanger the peace then and
there, to deprave public morality generally, to shake the fabric of
society and to be a cause of civil strife'.

In theory, at least, the blasphemy laws are still the main means
whereby Christianity is protected against obscene or violent abuse.
In practice, however, as has already been noted, the law began to
fall into disuse during the 1920s. In 1949 Lord Denning declared it
obsolete and at the same time consigned the floodgate-theory to the
history books:

> The reason for this law was because it was thought that a denial
> of Christianity was liable to shake the fabric of society, which was
> itself founded upon Christian religion. There is no such danger to
> society now and the offence of blasphemy is a dead letter.

Although the offence of blasphemy was revived by Mary
Whitehouse during the *Gay News* trial, Lord Denning's view has
found a considerable degree of acceptance in legal circles, as seems
to be borne out by the Law Commission Report of 1985.

So far the account of the blasphemy laws which I have given here
follows the International Committee's document quite closely, and
some of the examples and quotations I have used are culled directly
from it. This is because I find myself in almost complete agreement
with one of its lines of argument. Indeed, although the document
is extremely one-sided and although it passes over many crucial
facts in silence, it does perform a useful function by reminding us
of the continually recurring episodes of religious repression which
most liberal historians prefer to forget, but which are part of our
own history, and which are therefore part of the history of
democracy itself.

Where I find myself parting company with the authors of the International Committee's document is when they move from the past to the future and suggest that the abolition of the blasphemy laws would in itself bring about on the one hand a significant increase in individual liberty, and on the other hand a significant increase in religious equality. The basis of my disagreement is very simple. For what students of blasphemy law have almost always failed to observe is that the seeming obsolescence of the blasphemy laws does not indicate simply that we have grown out of them. Both in cultural and in psychological terms, it might be a great deal more accurate to suggest that we have grown *into* them, and that, behind the change in legal attitudes towards blasphemy, there lies a profound process of cultural and psychological internalisation.

Such a process of internalisation is unlikely ever to be complete. But, to a certain degree at least, it seems reasonable to argue that respect for the figure of Jesus and for Christianity in general has been inculcated so widely, even among non-believers, that the restraints of good taste have gradually made the restraints of the law all but redundant. In any ordinary social relationship it would be considered an unpardonable breach of good taste for a sceptic or a non-believer to engage in obscene blasphemies against Jesus or against the Christian faith in the presence of a devout Christian. So profoundly do we seem to have internalised the sacredness of the Christian religion that such blasphemies would probably be considered distasteful even if they were uttered only in the company of fellow sceptics or unbelievers. Indeed, it is probably true to say that the majority of British people, whether or not they have had a religious upbringing, would find it psychologically difficult to engage in extreme or obscene blasphemy even in the privacy of their own imaginations.

It is perhaps partly because of such internalised repression that the role of artists, poets, novelists and film-makers as 'agents' of blasphemy has become so important in the twentieth century. Imaginative artists have, in effect, been licensed to engage in blasphemy on behalf of those who, because of their own relative imaginative rigidity, find it difficult to do so. But even the licence we give to artists to blaspheme is itself severely limited. Occasional blasphemies can be tolerated in the confidence that their example is unlikely to be followed; there is no longer a danger of the floodgates of impiety springing open. But extreme or obscene blasphemy is still effectively outlawed or restricted to special contexts. It is quite true that this kind of restriction is not normally regulated by invoking the law. But here once again we encounter the results of a process of cultural internalisation. Because of this process individuals or organisations can, to a large extent, be relied upon to impose the kind of censorship which was once enforced by the state.

In this respect we would do well to remember that *The Satanic Verses* is not the only Penguin book which has been burnt in recent years. Not many years ago almost the entire print-run of a Penguin book was burnt on the grounds that its contents were blasphemous and would be deeply offensive to many Christians in this country. The book in question was Siné's *Massacre*. Siné is one of France's most acclaimed cartoonists. Much of his work makes satirical forays into the realms of sexual behaviour, scatology and religion and his cartoons often have an anti-clerical theme. *Massacre* by and large eschews his explicit and extremely funny sexual satire, but it does contain a number of scatological, anti-clerical or blasphemous cartoons, some of them with a sexual theme. The Penguin edition of *Massacre* was introduced by Malcolm Muggeridge and published in 1967 at the time that Penguin was under the direction of Tony Godwin. Many booksellers, however, found the book deeply offensive because of its blasphemous content and some conveyed their feelings to Allen Lane, who had by this time almost retired from Penguin Books. His response was swift and effective. One night, soon after the book had been published, he went into Penguin's Harmondsworth warehouse with four accomplices, filled a trailer with all the remaining copies of the book, drove away and burnt them. The next day the Penguin trade department reported the book 'out of print'. Allen Lane took this action not because he was a practising Christian himself, but because many of his friends and bookselling colleagues were, and had conveyed to him their strong distaste for the book.

Of course it may be argued that Allen Lane was wrong to act in this way. But given that he did it would be almost hypocritical not to recall his action now. For it places the present controversy over the *Satanic Verses* in a much needed perspective. It reminds us above all that in this country the authority of the Church and the sensitivities of individual Christians are protected not so much by the force of law but – far more significantly – by the manner in which ancient and seemingly obsolete blasphemy laws have been internalised. As a result, powerful organisations – or individuals like Allen Lane – frequently intervene in the publishing process in order to moderate, edit, or indeed suppress works which might be considered blasphemous.

In 1976, nearly ten years after Allen Lane's dramatic intervention in the case of *Massacre*, a significant controversy developed around the Danish film-maker Jens Jorgen Thorsen, who was planning a film about the sex-life of Jesus, *The Many Faces of Jesus*, involving both homosexual and heterosexual acts. His proposal to make the film in Britain met with intense opposition which was eventually successful. This opposition came not only from pressure groups but also from the Queen, the Prime Minister, James Callaghan, and the Archbishop of Canterbury, Donald Coggan.

A similar kind of internalised censorship played a significant role in the handling of the Monty Python team's controversial film *The Life of Brian* (1979). As a satire on religion, this film might well be considered a rather slight production. As blasphemy it was, even in its original version, extremely mild. Yet the film was surrounded from its inception by intense anxiety, in some quarters of the Establishment, about the offence it might cause. As a result it gained a certificate for general release only after some cuts had been made. Perhaps more importantly still, the film was shunned by BBC and ITV, who declined to show it for fear of offending Christians in this country. Once again a blasphemy was restrained – or its circulation effectively curtailed – not by the force of law but by the internalisation of this law.

The action which Allen Lane took in 1967, the successful campaign against *The Many Faces of Jesus*, and the partial suppression of *The Life of Brian* tell part of the story of the way in which attitudes towards blasphemy have evolved in our society. But it is not the whole story. A far more telling perspective on the status of blasphemy is offered if we consider the manner in which, in our once theocratic state, the authority of the individual conscience has gradually been accorded the same position, and been veiled with the same sanctity, as the authority of the scriptures in earlier centuries.

The elevation of the individual conscience and the manner in which we now defer to its authority is one of the most important parts of our Puritan inheritance. Whereas the medieval Roman Catholic Church had developed a vast apparatus of external authority, and a complex ecclesiastical hierarchy by which all individual believers were bound, Puritans regarded external authority with distaste, and placed great emphasis instead on inner discipline. One of the great ideals of the Puritan movement, deriving from St Paul – who had in turn derived it from Old Testament prophets like Ezekiel – was that the laws of God should be written not upon tablets of stone, but upon the individual heart of every true believer. The believer's lawful heart would then become his Christian conscience, and this conscience would become the ultimate religious authority. The Pope would, as it were, be humbly enthroned in the ordinary palace of every individual soul and would there become the infallible arbiter of God's will, which would be performed, not because of some external discipline but because of an inner compulsion.

As the Puritan movement developed, the radical implications of the new conscience-centred attitude towards Christian doctrine gradually began to emerge. John Milton was one of many seventeenth-century Puritans who, basing his arguments in part on the corrupt and distorted nature of the text of the Bible, rejected it as an infallible guide to the will of God. According to this view, the authority of the Bible was to be subordinated to what Puritans were wont to call 'the Christ within'. For Milton, the ultimate court of appeal always remained that of reason or the inner conscience. If a particular passage of the scriptures could not be reconciled with the cause of human or moral good, then it was to be rejected: 'No ordinance,' said Milton, 'human or from heaven, can bind against the good of man.' 'Milton', writes Christopher Hill, 'was glad to find that ideas which he arrived at by searching his own conscience could be found in the Bible; but they had greater authority for him because they were in his conscience than because they were in the Bible.' The same principle was widely upheld by other radical Puritans. Jacob Bauthumely did not 'expect to be taught by Bibles or books but by God'. 'The Bible without,' he wrote, 'is but a shadow of the Bible which is within.'

The implications of this conscience-centred revolution for the crime of blasphemy were far-reaching indeed, and continue to make themselves felt today. As long as the Bible continued to be regarded as the ultimate authority in matters of faith, any attempt to quarrel with the sacred word or with the traditional biblical images of God was anathema and was vigorously condemned. But gradually, as the conscience-centred revolution deepened during the sixteenth and seventeenth centuries, a conflict began to grow between the old scriptural images of God and the new demands of the internalised conscience. Although, as we have seen, the state continued rigorously to enforce the law against blasphemy, it frequently found itself in conflict not with scoffers, unbelievers or atheists but with devout Puritans whose main crime was not that they rejected Christ, but that they rejected the Christ of the scriptures in order to follow the 'Christ-within'. Indeed blasphemy, or attitudes which verged on blasphemy, even began to have a certain theological attraction for some of the most rigorous and conscientious Puritans. According to Gerrard Winstanley, any traditional Christian, 'who thinks God is in the heavens above the skies, and so prays to that god which he imagines to be there and everywhere ....worships his own imagination, which is the devil'. Elsewhere Winstanley refers almost contemptuously to 'the outward Christ and the outward God' and goes on to speak of 'the God Devil'. In 1646 another Puritan, John Boggis of Great Yarmouth, asked, 'Where is your God, in Heaven or in earth, aloft or below, or where doth he sit with his arse?'

The trial of James Nayler in 1656, which has already been referred to, is a perfect example of this trend. For Nayler's alleged claim of equality with God was precisely the kind of claim which proceeded logically out of the Puritan enthronement of the conscience. The blasphemous Nayler, and the Quaker sect to which he belonged, were among the chief pioneers of the 'internalised Christianity' which would increasingly be adopted as an orthodoxy in Protestant England. In one sense, indeed, it would seem that blasphemy provided some of the most rigid Puritans with a necessary psychological path away from a traditional scriptural Christianity towards a new religion of the conscience; it was only by pelting the traditional scriptural image of God – the 'Christ without' – with the stones of irreverence and blasphemy, that they were able to 'kill off' the old form of religious authority and make room for a new form.

This religious appropriation of blasphemy is by no means only a feature of our Puritan past, for in some significant respects it continues today. Theologically speaking, the heirs to Gerrard Winstanley and John Boggis are men like Bishop Robinson and Bishop Jenkins. The books which they, and the other new theologians of Puritanism have written, are earnest and utterly sincere attempts to make private doubts public and, by doing so, to be 'honest to God'. But their books are at the same time violent, and at times quite extraordinarily insensitive attacks on the traditional scriptural image of God which many ordinary Christians continue to worship and from which they continue to draw immense psychological comfort. In terms of any traditional Christian view, the vision of these new theologians is not simply radical or revolutionary. It verges on blasphemy and is profoundly threatening. It is little wonder that so many Christians have found books such as *Honest to God* so hurtful.

In liberal intellectual circles, however, there is scant sympathy for such Christians and a great deal of fellow-feeling for the radical theologians who have so scandalised them. In view of this, and in view of the way in which we have virtually enthroned blasphemy as an orthodox part of modern Christian theology, it is scarcely surprising that we find it so difficult to understand the feelings of the countless thousands of ordinary Muslims who are outraged by *The Satanic Verses*.

That feeling of outrage, however, is in most cases utterly genuine and quite independent of the Ayatollah Khomeini's death-threat against Salman Rushdie. It is felt so strongly for the simple reason that the major part of the Islamic world has never passed through the same kind of conscience-centred revolution which is such an important part of our own historical experience. Islam has never established the primacy and the sanctity of the 'God-within' and most ordinary Muslims have not developed any attitude which parallels the Puritan notion of 'a Bible-within'. The Koran remains the essential and only sanctuary of God and of the Prophet Muhammad, and any attempt to tamper with that sanctuary or to abuse its holiness is seen as an attempt to destroy religion itself. As Amir Taheri has written: 'Most Muslims are prepared to be broad-minded about most things but never about anything which even remotely touches upon their faith. "Better that I be dead than see Islam insulted," said Ayatollah Majlisi in the last century. An Arab proverb says: "Kill me, but do not mock my faith".'

It is because the faith of ordinary Muslims relies so heavily on external authority and on the sacred tradition of the Koran, and because they identify this tradition with all that is precious and emotionally rich, that they are prepared to defend the sanctity of the Koran and of the figure of the Prophet with such passion and such apparent rigidity. It is this seeming rigidity which has in its turn evoked the fury of many liberal intellectuals who believe that their own rights to free expression are being infringed or destroyed.

By placing this conflict in a historical context I hope I have made it clear that one argument which is commonly advanced about *The Satanic Verses* is unsound. For it is emphatically not true that British people enjoy now, or have ever enjoyed, an unlimited liberty to blaspheme against the Christian faith. Since Christianity is protected not only by the law but also by a whole series of taboos which have been profoundly internalised, and since modern 'death-of-God theology' has tended to appropriate blasphemy for its own religious ends, abolition of the current blasphemy laws would *not* have the effect of placing all religions in this country on an equal footing. It would simply render the current state of religious inequality more invisible. By banishing a palpable injustice in order to ratify an impalpable injustice, it would almost certainly leave the Muslim community in this country, as well as some other religious minorities, feeling more precarious and more threatened.

To say this, however, does not in itself resolve any of the most important questions which have been raised by the publication of *The Satanic Verses* and by the Muslim response to it. For the fact that Muslims – or for that matter any other group of people – might feel threatened, discomforted or offended by the publication of a novel is not in itself a reason for suppressing that novel or declining to publish it in a paperback edition. Truth itself is sometimes painful, disturbing and offensive. That being so, the question which remains unanswered is whether blasphemy can itself be a vehicle of truth, and whether the right to engage in blasphemy against a particular religion, or indeed against all religions, is therefore a precious right which should be defended at all costs. In order to answer that question, I believe that we need to locate it not in some hypothetical Utopia but in the real historical and political world.

There are a number of situations in which the right to blaspheme would indeed appear to be worth defending. In any society where a tyrannical state authority is kept in place by a policy of religious terror, then blasphemy might well be seen as an important political act; by keeping alive the possibility of dissent it subverts the state's power and, perhaps, makes liberation more likely.

In Calvin's Geneva – which John Knox once called 'the most perfect school of Christ that ever was on earth since the days of the Apostles' – even the lightest action was brought under a rigid spiritual rule. Drunkards, dancers and adulterers were excommunicated, torture was used systematically, a child was beheaded for striking its parents and, in sixty years, one hundred and fifty men and women who had transgressed against Calvin's spiritual discipline were burnt at the stake. Calvin, in the words of R.H.Tawney, 'made Geneva a city of glass, in which every household lived its life under the supervision of a spiritual police'. In such a city it might indeed seem that blasphemy offered a road to liberation, and that any God who was invoked to justify such terror should be treated with open and systematic disrespect.

Much the same might be said of Russia during the time of Stalin. For although Stalin's regime was not sustained by any orthodox form of religion, Stalin so managed the cult of his own personality that he himself effectively became the 'God' of a tyrannical state-religion, surrounding his own image with reverence, fear and the holy terror which would eventually claim the lives of at least thirty million Soviet citizens. Dissidence, in such circumstances, demanded a healthy disrespect for the god-like image Stalin sought to project and once again it might be argued that any form of 'blasphemy', however scurrilously it abused Stalin, could be justified politically as a step along the road to liberation.

I have introduced these two examples quite deliberately, however, in order to show that, although blasphemy may sometimes appear to be desirable, it is not always politically expedient. For tyrants who use religious terror in order to impose their own forms of political discipline do not make exceptions of blasphemers; they make examples of them. In Calvin's Geneva blasphemers, like all other religious dissidents, were put to death.

In Stalin's Russia anyone so misguided as to show in public the slightest sign of disrespect for Stalin himself would almost certainly be arrested and either executed or tortured into submission. It is certainly true that cursing God privately in Calvin's Geneva or cursing Stalin during the time of the Great Purge might well have provided individual dissidents with necessary psychological relief; at times furtive blasphemies exchanged by dissidents might even have become the secret and necessary opium of dissent. But public blasphemy was a quite different matter. Those who engaged in it were not committing acts of political courage; they were committing an act of supreme political folly. At best they were throwing away valuable human resources by going to war with a strategically useless weapon. At worst they were actively strengthening the regime of the very tyrant they sought to oppose. For religious tyrants are almost always skilled at taking the scurrilous insults and obscenities which are associated with blasphemy and directing these back against the blasphemer. What happens, in effect, is that those who engage in blasphemy against repressive regimes provide those regimes with the very kind of unclean Antichrist they need in order to unite followers behind them and sustain and redouble their repressive zeal.

Blasphemy, then, when it is exercised by the powerless against the powerful, may *seem* to be be justifiable, but it is often politically destructive and it may have the effect of strengthening the authoritarianism of the regime which is attacked. In this respect it is very like violence or terrorism. Terrorist attacks on extreme repressive regimes may sometimes seem morally right, but they are not always advisable. This is partly because of the danger of detection, and partly because political violence can all too easily give a propaganda advantage to the enemy and allow a repressive state to fortify itself further against 'the enemy within'.

In the particular case of *The Satanic Verses*, we should have no doubt at all that Salman Rushdie's intention was to use blasphemy as a way of attacking unjustifiable forms of political and religious rigidity. In reality, however, it seems reasonably clear that his book has had precisely the opposite effect. For instead of leading to a significant weakening in the power structures of Islamic fundamentalism, the real and deeply felt offence caused by the book to many ordinary Muslims was actually seized upon by Khomeini to help shore up his own shaky political regime. At the same time many Muslims, above all in Britain, have been deflected from a path of religious moderation towards forms of extremism which had previously held no attraction for them. In this respect it would seem that Rushdie's own sophisticated insensitivity to the language of faith and to religious politics in general has actually played into the hands of fundamentalists. By allowing himself to be cast as a rigid and intolerant Antichrist-figure, surrounded and supported by the seemingly militant liberal armies of the West, he has effectively redoubled the very rigid zeal he set out in his book to diminish.

What is perhaps even more serious and more dangerous in this whole affair, however, has been the insensitivity of almost the entire Western intellectual establishment to some of the deepest imaginative currents of Judaeo-Christian and Islamic history and in particular to the role which has been played by blasphemy in the relationship between the three 'religions of Abraham'.

One of the reasons that this dimension of the problem has been ignored is that we tend to think of blasphemy as an essentially 'irreligious' act; indeed, until the *Satanic Verses* affair placed the whole subject in a wider context, blasphemy sometimes tended to be thought of as implying disrespect specifically for the Christian religion. It is this view which, as we have seen, is reflected in the British law on blasphemy. It is sometimes assumed that this law reflects a general antipathy to blasphemy of any kind, and that the specific and narrow application of the law is merely a historical accident. Such a view would certainly seem to correspond to the current position of the Church of England which, both through the Archbishop of Canterbury and through the Bishop of Bradford, has shown great restraint, wisdom and sensitivity throughout the Rushdie affair. If, however, we look at the problem of blasphemy in the long perspectives of history, we will find that the Christian church as a whole has generally interpreted the law against blasphemy in a quite different way. For, while fiercely resisting and punishing blasphemies directed against God, Christ or against the Christian faith in general, the church has at times actively encouraged Christians to engage in blasphemy, sometimes of a scurrilous and obscene kind, against rival faiths.

Historically, the main sufferers from such religiously motivated blasphemy have been Jews and Muslims. As Christian scholars have themselves now recognised, Western anti-semitism is a specifically Christian phenomenon which stems from the New

Testament itself – and not only from the writings of Paul, but also from the gospels, whose anti-Jewish bias is clear and consistent. In the twentieth century, anti-semitism has lost much of its religious colouring. In earlier centuries, however, the religious basis of anti-semitism was almost always clear and explicit. In his *Von den Juden*, to take but one example, Martin Luther condemned all Jews as greedy and maggoty: 'You are unworthy to look at the outside of the Bible, let alone read inside it. You should read only the Bible which is under the sow's tail, and gobble and guzzle the epistles which fall from it.' Luther went on to identify the sow with the Talmud and this idea was taken up by a fellow Christian, the Professor of Hebrew at Wittenberg University:

> What shall we say of the deep obtuseness of the Jews! The Son of God came to save his people, but they would not recognise him...They had been called and elected to be God's mouth, to fulfil God's word; but they closed their mouths to the flow of all the good from God and opened their mouths and all their sense to the Devil who filled them with...lies, impiety, blasphemy...The Rabbis, enemies of God and blasphemers against the Messiah and his most holy Mother...do not understand anything divine. Instead of the flowing water of eternal life, they suck the milk of a sow...they eat nothing...but excrement and dung...They take all their mysteries from the piggish Talmud, they suck all the impurity from the teats of swine. Thus cut off through incredulity from the olive and vine of Christ, they eagerly pursue only the most impure filthiness. Having deserted Christ they adhere to a sow; having despised the doctrines of the messiah, they devour dung; having neglected the word of life, they suck in their muddy milk...

The pronouncements of Martin Luther and his Christian colleague at the University of Wittenberg were, we should not doubt, motivated by a passionate devotion to the Christian faith and to the teachings of Jesus. Their purpose was to defend this faith against those who seemed to threaten it and to do so in terms which would be approved by Jesus, who had Himself, according to the gospel of John, anathematised all Jews as 'children of the devil'. Yet it will be clear to almost all modern observers that these 'holy' words are also profoundly blasphemous, and that contemporary Jews would have found them deeply hurtful and offensive to their religious faith.

This particular kind of Christian anti-semitism uses one of the commonest of anti-semitic motifs – that of the *Judensau* or Jews' Sow. This form of anti-Jewish insult, in which Jews were portrayed sucking on the teats of a sow or greedily eating its excrement, was central to Christian anti-semitism in Germany for more than three centuries. The motif was eventually secularised by National Socialists, and made one of its last appearances in 1937 in the form of a cartoon in Julius Streicher's anti-semitic newspaper *Der Stürmer*. More generally, scurrilous and obscene blasphemies directed against Jews and against Jewish forms of religious observance, or against Muslims and their faith, have formed one of the most significant elements in Christian apologetics for very many centuries.

Nor would it be fair to see this tendency to exploit or idealise sectarian blasphemy as an exclusively Christian phenomenon. For the systematic use of blasphemy lies close to the imaginative heart of the writings of the Old Testament prophets. Again and again the zeal which is shown by these prophets to serve the God of Israel goes hand in hand with their rage to denounce the gods of every other religion – especially the religion of the Canaanites – as inferior and evil. Specifically, prophets such as Amos, Ezekiel and Jeremiah introduced into Western religion the notion that any form of religious faith which set itself up against the pure cult of Yahweh was to be imagined in obscene terms as a prostitute, and its adherents reviled accordingly. It was this idea which was taken up in late Jewish and Christian apocalyptic and developed, through the figure of the Whore of Babylon, into one of the central motifs of all sectarian conflict within the Judaeo-Christian tradition.

It is because a tradition of violent and obscene blasphemy lies so close to the heart of Judaeo-Christian orthodoxy – and to Judaeo-Christian authoritarianism – that those who play imaginative games with blasphemy in the name of liberty are in reality engaged in an extraordinarily dangerous ploy, whose ultimate effect may be both destructive and repressive. The greatest danger of all is that their own blasphemies will be construed as belonging to the strongest tradition of Western blasphemy – a tradition which is both profoundly authoritarian and full of racial and religious hatred.

It is exactly this which appears to have happened in the reception of *The Satanic Verses*. In this regard it should hardly be necessary to point out that the Rushdie affair is not an isolated skirmish in an otherwise harmonious relationship between Islam and the West. It is rather the latest battle in a long history of religious and cultural tension which goes back to the seventh century, when Islam first emerged as a religion with the power to challenge Christendom. This tension was expressed in its most destructive form in the Crusades, during which hundreds of thousands of Muslims were killed by Western zealots. The Crusaders' bitter legacy to the Christian West, for whose supremacy they fought, was a dramatic intensification of traditional Christian anti-semitism. This new, intensified anti-semitism was expressed both against Jews and against Muslims. Partly because it was older and had its roots deep in the New Testament, it was anti-Jewish hatred which became most strongly established in Western Europe. And for geographical and demographical reasons, as well as for historical reasons, it was anti-Jewish prejudice which became one of the most decisive forces in European history during the eighteenth and nineteenth centuries and the early part of the twentieth century.

Throughout this period, however, the ancient hostility to Islam was kept alive. This hostility was so deep partly because it was based on a real power-struggle for control of Europe. The Arab invasion of Western Europe was stopped only at the battle of Tours in 712. But the military and political threat which Islam posed to Christendom continued. The Turks were halted at Vienna as late as 1683 and even after this, until the collapse of the Ottoman Empire after the First World War, some parts of what had once been Christendom remained under Turkish rule. Christian fears of Islam, then, were based in part on a real perception of its military, political and cultural strength. But the tendency of Christians to demonise their enemies meant that realistic fears of Islam were increasingly overlaid by demonological fantasies in which Muslims in general, and Muhammad in particular, were seen as satanic beings.

Throughout almost the whole of Christian Europe these fantasies about Muslims developed alongside much more powerful demonological fantasies about Jews. During the nineteenth and twentieth centuries both fantasies were gradually rationalised in secular terms, on the one hand by theorists of race, and on the other hand by orientalists. When, in the face of the deeds of Hitler's Germany, Christian and post-Christian Europe began to recoil in horror from its tradition of anti-Jewish prejudice, there was no parallel diminution in its ancient tradition of hatred for Islam. Indeed one of the changes which began to take place in the cultural imagination of the West was a gradual displacement of prejudice from Judaism to Islam – from Jews to Muslims and Arabs.

With the notable exception of Karen Armstrong, whose profound study of the religious origins of the Middle East conflict, *Holy War*, deserves to be better known than it is, most Western commentators seem scarcely to have noted this disturbing historical process, still less analysed it. But it has been observed by some who are themselves more closely involved in the conflict. In 1973, at the time of the OPEC crisis, the Palestinian literary critic Edward Said noticed the appearance in America of cartoons depicting an Arab standing beside a petrol pump:

> These Arabs, however, were clearly 'Semitic': their sharply-hooked noses, the evil, mustachioed leer on their faces, were obvious reminders (to a largely non-Semitic population) that 'Semites' were at the bottom of all 'our' troubles, which in this case was principally a gasoline shortage. The transference of a popular anti-Semitic animus from a Jewish to an Arab target was made smoothly, since the figure was essentially the same.

Quoting Said's words, Karen Armstrong comments that 'this is a precisely observed example of the frightening fact that the hatred we used to allow ourselves to feel about the Jews has been transferred *in toto* to the "Arab"'. She goes on to observe that this new kind of racial stereotyping is particularly dangerous now that the Arabs are seen as the enemies of the Jews and the new anti-semites:

> Much of our new prejudice is a transfer of unmanageable guilt. The Arab is being made to carry a double load of hatred in Europe: besides bearing the traditional Western hatred of the 'Muslim', he is now having to take on our load of guilt for our...anti-semitism.

Recognition of this new and potent form of prejudice is necessary, I believe, if we are to understand the extraordinary violence of the Muslim reaction to the treatment of Islam in Salman Rushdie's *The Satanic Verses*.

To the casual Western observer the *Satanic Verses* affair seemed, in its early stages at least, a more or less internal squabble in which a Muslim writer, who happened to live in a Western country, was being reviled for daring to attack, in a distinctively modern way, the religious faith in which he had been brought up. Since Islam was perceived by such observers as a uniquely cruel and repressive religion, it tended to be assumed automatically that Rushdie's blasphemies were offered in the name of life, liberty and imaginative exuberance. To most Muslims, however, Rushdie's offence is quite different. For some of the passages from *The Satanic Verses* which they find most offensive draw on motifs and on characterisations of Muhammad which are not modern at all. They belong rather to the ancient tradition of religiously inspired contempt for Islam which was nurtured by the Christian Church in the West throughout countless centuries. It is from this tradition and its secular transformations that Rushdie draws the character of his Muhammad-figure, Mahound. As a result, the prophet emerges from Rushdie's novel as an insincere businessman, 'a calculating opportunist devoid of conscience, making and breaking rules as he pleases, confusing (or perhaps deliberately identifying) good with evil as the mood takes him'. The words are those of Shabbir Akhtar. In his book, *Be Careful With Muhammad!*, Akhtar goes on to expound some of the more general Muslim complaints about Rushdie's novel:

> *The Satanic Verses* is written in a language that is at times gratuitously obscene and wounding. In the controversial sections about Mahound, the locales Rushdie selects are almost always sexually suggestive...and sometimes even degrade human nature. Much of the abuse, though, is straightforwardly explicit. Bilal, Khalid and Salman, who are three of Mahound's most distinguished companions, emerge as drunkards, idlers and fools, 'the trinity of scum', 'that bunch of riff raff', 'fucking clowns'. Mahound himself is portrayed as a debauched sensualist, a drunkard given to self-indulgence. He is depicted lying naked and unconscious in Hind's tent with a hangover...
>
> There is a sustained attack on values such as chastity and modesty too. In a brothel, provocatively called *The Veil*, the prostitutes assume the names and roles of Mahound's wives. The anti-Islamic poet Baal becomes the husband of the wives of the 'businessman prophet'...
>
> The brothel scene is of course purely imaginary; even Christian polemicists have drawn the line at this kind of insult. Unlike his Western supporters, Rushdie himself writes with an insider's awareness of the outrage such a portrayal would cause.

Muhammad's spouses are instructed, by the Koran, to remain unmarried after their husband's death, so that they can assume the honorific title, 'the mothers of the believers'. Muslims have reacted to what they take to be a straightforward personal attack.

Frequently Western intellectuals have attempted to dismiss such Muslim reactions as the product merely of prudishness or sexual repression. This is scarcely fair since, though Islam clearly has its own forms of puritanism, it is no more anti-sexual than Judaism, and a good deal less so than Christianity. As Akhtar himself writes, 'It is not as though we have over a million Mary Whitehouses among us'. The Muslim objection is not, at root, an objection to the sexualisation or the eroticisation of the Prophet. For that is not how the relevant passages of the novel are perceived. They are perceived as an attempt to use obscenity not to enrich but to smear. The objection is not to sex but to the use of sex as a form of vilification. Nor should it be assumed that this kind of reaction is peculiar to Muslims. For it was a very similar reaction which, some ten years ago, triggered the campaign against Jens Jorgen Thorsen's film *The Many Faces of Jesus*. British Muslims, it would seem, have much in common with a former Prime Minister, a former Archbishop of Canterbury and the Queen.

It must be said, however, that Muslims have very good reasons to be especially sensitive to such treatment of their own sacred figures. For both Christian polemicists and Western orientalists sought for centuries to denigrate Islam by attributing to it a fantastic, disreputable or demonic sexuality. And what almost all Muslims know, from their intuitive grasp of their own history, is that there is nothing remotely liberating in this kind of Western fantasy. For in the past such fantasies have always tended to belong to the propaganda which has preceded the sword, the bullet and the bomb. What Muslims see in Rushdie's fictional adaptations of ancient stereotypes is not simply hatred, but the long, terrible, triumphalist hatred which the West has had for Islam almost since its beginnings.

To find such hateful stereotypes revived not by one of their traditional enemies, but by a writer who was himself born to a Muslim family in Bombay, is especially hurtful. When ordinary Muslims in this country see that writer richly repaid for his irreverence, feted and celebrated both by intellectuals and by the Western media, while they are rewarded for their faith with ill-disguised contempt, it is little wonder that they feel betrayed in the most intimate and cruel manner, and feel at the same time that their own future existence, security and safety in the West is threatened. Given all this, it should not be surprising that Muslims in this country reacted to the publication of Rushdie's book in the way that they did, and that a number of them wrote in passionate terms to Penguin Books pleading for the book's withdrawal. It is not surprising either that, when these passionate pleas failed to produce any real response, these Muslims should have resorted to more dramatic methods, burning the book in public in an attempt to interest the media in their campaign.

Nor is it entirely surprising that, when they succeeded and Western intellectuals, journalists and writers rose in order to condemn them and to defend democracy and its freedoms, Muslims responded by redoubling their campaign. For, as at least one Muslim spokesman pointed out at the time, one of the most precious rights in any democracy is freedom of association. In availing themselves of that freedom and of their entirely legal right to demonstrate against a book by which they felt insulted, they were simply using the very democratic liberties their critics claimed to be defending. Moreover, possessing still the visceral sense of history which Western intellectuals have destroyed, most Muslims knew all too well what this Western passion for freedom had meant in terms of their own history. They knew that the cutting edge of the Western conscience was a sword, and that democracy usually appeared in the form of an invading army.

The sceptical anger of many Muslims when they are faced by Western cries of democracy and conscience is perhaps best expressed in the words of the young Syrian writer, Rana Kabbani:

> Is the Western conscience not selective? The West feels sympathy for the Afghan Mujahedin, propped up by American intelligence just as the Nicaraguan Contras were, but feels no sympathy for militant Muslims who are not fighting its cold war battles but have political concerns of their own. As I write, Palestinians are dying every day in the Occupied Territories – nearly 600 dead at the latest count, over 30,000 wounded and 20,000 in detention without trial – savage and prolonged curfews are imposed as routine collective punishments, homes are blown up, pregnant women gassed and beaten and unarmed boys kicked to death by regular soldiers, yet Israel remains a democracy in Western eyes, an

outpost of Western civilisation. What is one to think of such double standards?

Considering these circumstances it is not surprising that an extremist political Islam has taken root all over the world, fuelled by historical grievance, by poverty, by an overriding sense of powerlessness. The West bears more than a measure of responsibility for this phenomenon. For by interfering so forcefully in Muslim affairs, by overthrowing nationalist rulers (as was done in Iran, for example, in 1953) and setting up puppets in their place, by uncritical support for Israeli excesses, by milking Muslim resources and conspiring to keep the Muslim world economically, culturally and politically enthralled, the West has made us what we are: enraged and unforgiving.

It is the long history of humiliation which Kabbani recalls here which helps to explain the intensity of the rage with which Muslims responded to *The Satanic Verses*.

Perhaps the most unfortunate aspect of the entire Rushdie affair was that this Muslim rage tended to be met not with the moderation which liberal intellectuals preached but with their own more sophisticated forms of rage. It is true that some individuals and organisations responded in a very different manner. A very few, such as the Commission for Racial Equality and the Inter Faith Network, made immensely constructive efforts to bring about a real dialogue between the various participants in the debate. But in the immediate aftermath of the *fatwa* this represented a minority response. Indeed a number of intellectuals and writers made the situation a great deal worse by resorting to forms of anti-intellectualism, in which careful analysis was eschewed in favour of the reflex chanting of the slogans and shibboleths of liberalism. Christopher Hitchens, who is often a cogent and perceptive cultural critic, made the following speech during the course of a rally of American writers:

> As writers and *soi-disant* intellectuals, it is most often our job to stress complexity, to point out with care and attention that 'it's not as simple as that'. But there are also times when it is irresponsible not to stress the essential clarity and simplicity of a question. The almost boastful threat to murder not just a book but an author is one such time. Moments of this sort have a galvanizing effect on our standby phrases and our most cherished clichés...

Other writers have responded in a way which has both revived and intensified the relatively new form of religious and racial hatred which we have just examined.

For confirmation of this we only have to look at some of the responses which the Rushdie affair has evoked from those who might once have been regarded as 'liberals'. In her Counterblast pamphlet on the Rushdie affair, *Sacred Cows*, we are treated to the remarkable spectacle of Fay Weldon endorsing the Bible as a sound basis for a society while, in the same breath, she condemns the Koran:

> The Koran is food for no-thought. It is not a poem on which society can be safely or sensibly based. It gives weapons and strength to the thought-police – and the thought-police are easily set marching and they frighten...You can build a decent society around the Bible...but the Koran? No.

This passage is quoted by Rana Kabbani in her own recent contribution to the Rushdie debate, *Letter to Christendom*. Understandably enough Kabbani reproves Fay Weldon both for her 'cultural arrogance' and her 'rash judgments'. She then quotes the even more remarkable words of Conor Cruise O'Brien in a review published in the *The Times* in May 1989:

> Muslim society looks profoundly repulsive...It looks repulsive because it is repulsive...A Westerner who claims to admire Muslim society, while still adhering to Western values, is either a hypocrite or an ignoramus, or a bit of both. At the heart of the matter is the Muslim family, an abominable institution....Arab and Muslim society is sick, and has been sick for a long time. In the last century the Arab thinker Jamal al-Afghani wrote: 'Every Muslim is sick and his only remedy is in the Koran.' Unfortunately the sickness gets worse the more the remedy is taken.

Having quoted these contemptuous and racist words, which were written by a former Editor-in-Chief of the *Observer*, but which could not conceivably have been published in a British newspaper before the Rushdie affair, Kabbani goes on to discuss the sense of grievance felt by Muslims because of their experience over the centuries of being colonised, manipulated and despised. 'In today's scale of values,' she writes, 'a Muslim life seems to weigh a good deal less than a Christian or a Jewish life.' These words are chilling, I suspect, precisely because they express a truth which it is taboo to utter. Kabbani herself eventually comes to a conclusion very similar to that which I have already suggested:

> I have come to think that anti-semitism, endemic in western culture, has more or less been forced underground. Thankfully, and for good historical reasons it is no longer easy to attack Jews publicly or depict them in fiction as unpleasant caricatures. But these salutary taboos do not extend to Muslims. I would even be so bold as to argue that there has been a transfer of contempt from Jews to Muslims in secular Western culture today. Many Muslims share this fear: indeed, one has written that 'the next time there are gas chambers in Europe, there is no doubt concerning who'll be inside them'.

The words which Kabbani quotes are those of Shabbir Akhtar, in an article in the *Guardian*. These words may seem to exaggerate the predicament of European Muslims. But, whether or not this is the case, I am quite sure that they reflect, as accurately as any of the words which have been spilt during the current controversy, how it sometimes feels to be a Muslim in the middle of secular Europe in the latter part of the twentieth century. Nor should we rule out the possibility that Akhtar, far from exaggerating, is actually showing a terrible prescience.

CHAPTER TWO

Liberalism's Holy War

If there has indeed been, in Rana Kabbani's words, a 'transfer of contempt' from Jews to Muslims in secular culture since 1945, and if Western blasphemies against Islam are having the effect of intensifying this process, then this still does not add up to an argument either for suppressing *The Satanic Verses* or for restraining its publication in any way – by withholding a paperback edition, for example. For the belief in 'freedom of expression' is an extremely powerful one. It is as precious to the West, almost, as the Koran itself is to Islam. It would be both foolish and insensitive to expect Western liberals to lay aside their most precious belief, simply because somebody's feelings are being hurt – or even because deep distress is being caused to an entire culture.

It must be said, however, that, like every other question in this debate, the whole issue of freedom of expression is a complex one – a great deal more complex and many-sided than the black-and-white views favoured by some would suggest.

Some of the most elementary objections to the liberal position have already been made many times during the course of the *Satanic Verses* debate. But no harm can be done by repeating those objections here.

For a start it is wrong to imply, as some artists and intellectuals seem to, that all attempts to bridle the way in which people express opinions are necessarily harmful. The Race Relations Act stops people from using words in order to incite racial hatred. It thus imposes a form of censorship. But it is not for that reason wrong. For a long time it has been illegal to incite people to murder. That, too, is a restraint on our freedom of speech which we would be unwise to dispense with. The law of libel is another far more sweeping restraint on freedom of speech. Sometimes the effect of this law is to suppress truths which should be told. But no civilised, democratic country would ever consider simply sweeping that law away. For words are not, as is sometimes claimed, neutral and harmless instruments. They can be as lethal, almost, as bullets and can cause great offence and personal distress. That is why absolute freedom of speech is ultimately no more desirable than absolute freedom to murder.

For centuries most democratic countries have recognised this and they have framed laws whose specific purpose is to constrain freedom of speech. Some of these laws are good, some, arguably, are bad. But one of the difficulties we have had throughout the duration of the *Satanic Verses* controversy is that a significant minority of artists and intellectuals appear to have succumbed to the liberal-democratic myth that none of these laws exist, that the purpose of democracies is to remove constraints on freedom and that our own democracy accords to all its members some absolute freedom of expression which is now under threat.

Whenever these same artists and intellectuals offer examples of this freedom of expression, they almost always draw them – understandably enough – from their own experience of artistic or intellectual activity. It is for this reason that their arguments tend to be so persuasive. For it is undeniably true that artists, novelists and intellectuals in modern Western societies *are* now accorded a degree of freedom which is extraordinary and unprecedented.

What is too rarely remarked on, however, is that this freedom is enjoyed only in extremely restricted contexts. One particular area of freedom which twentieth-century liberals have fought hard to establish is that found in the modern novel. The publication of *Ulysses* and the trial of *Lady Chatterley's Lover* are two of the more celebrated episodes in what has been a continuing story of reform designed to win for the novelist a seemingly complete freedom of vocabulary and subject-matter – particularly with regard to the portrayal of sexual love. We should not for a moment conclude, however, that this story of reform indicates that we have moved into an area of unrestrained liberty. For while it is certainly true that sexual attitudes *have* changed in the twentieth century, we only have to consider the obscenities which Lawrence used in his art to realise that some changes have been far from radical. For these obscenities are no less obscene now than they were when Lawrence used them. If anything, indeed, they are charged with an even more intense horror and fear than they were then, and express a yet more violent loathing of the human body and of sexual love than they ever did. It may well be that in a certain compartment of society, obscene words are used a little more frequently and more fearlessly than they once were. It is even the case that they have recently been heard on the radio in a reading of *Lady Chatterley's Lover*. But the extraordinary nature of this occasion is, in itself, a reflection of just how narrow and precarious is the 'freedom' which we appear to have won. For you only have to make a list of all the once-forbidden words and then recite this list to a policeman in a public place in the presence of one or two people of a censorious disposition and you will soon find yourself before a magistrate. And if *The Sunday Times*, or indeed most daily newspapers, reported your arrest they would most certainly decline to print in full – and without asterisks – the details of your crime. Nor for that matter would your transgression be accurately reported on BBC radio or discussed on BBC television. Unless, that is, the producer in question had first made a written application to the Director General and received formal permission.

Where, then, is our much vaunted freedom of speech? Where is the freedom to publish which we prize so much? The answer is that the freedom of expression we enjoy is very narrowly constrained indeed. This is one reason why the arguments about freeedom of expression, which liberals frequently advance in order to defend *The Satanic Verses*, are both ill-considered and, ultimately, dangerous. For these arguments are calmly advanced in a society where practically every medium of expression other than the novel is subject to the most complex and elaborate restrictions; where every programme that we watch on television has been vetted by guardians of public decency; where every film we see has been censored, and where the licence we extend to 'art' encourages us to forget that every 'non-artistic' picture ever published or displayed is subject to rigorous obscenity laws. These laws express, in their selective prohibitions and permissions, a seemingly profound antipathy to sexual love and a deep and almost insane horror of some of the most ordinary parts of the human body, particularly when these are conjoined in some of the most ordinary ways. Not only this, but in this same 'free' society, a law has recently been passed in which civil servants have been deprived of one of the most important freedoms which they had previously enjoyed under the law – the freedom to place the demands of conscience above the demands of their government.

If we are to have any hope of unravelling the terrible problems which have been brought to the surface of the liberal conscience by the publication of *The Satanic Verses*, we need first of all to recognise, however painful this may be, that we do *not* live in a free society, and that we do not generally enjoy freedom of expression.

Secondly we need to recognise that democracy itself is not synonymous with liberty and that in some very important respects it is antipathetic to liberty. For democracies are not built on accumulated layers of freedom; they are built upon the rule of law, which in its turn consists in the selective deprivation of freedom. In this respect it is quite wrong to see some absolute disjunction between totalitarian societies and democracies. The relationship between the two forms of government was perhaps best illuminated by one of George Orwell's remarks, in which he observed that the perfect totalitarian society was one whose citizens were so drilled to conformity that there was no need for a police force. The citizens of such a perfect totalitarian state would presumably be free in all outward respects. They would be free to express subversive opinions and formulate 'revolutionary' philosophies because these would almost certainly turn out to be disguised forms of authoritarianism. They would be free to engage in all manner of sexual activities in private, because the rule of puritanism and sex-hatred over public life would already be complete and would be relentlessly maintained by a puritanical 'free press' hungry for the titillation of scandals it felt duty bound to expose. They would be free to vote – for the simple reason that all the major political parties would be pale reflections or mirror-images of each other's conformity, who disagreed only about the different ways of managing the same structures of power.

The citizens of this perfect state would, in short, be free to do everything precisely because they were powerless to change anything. Most importantly of all, they would be free to blaspheme against the religion of the state. Indeed leaders of the perfect totalitarian state would rigorously protect the freedom of a tiny elite of artists and intellectuals to do just this. They would do so partly in order to perpetuate the myth of freedom which gave their regime legitimacy, but mainly because of their intuitive knowledge that, in a deeply conformist society, any criticism of the ruling ideology made in terms which are obscene, scurrilous, unruly or distasteful to the majority, actually has the effect of tightening social control and allowing ideological defences to be deepened.

The hypothetical perfect totalitarian society which I describe here does not exist. Nor is it likely, given the limitations of human nature, that it ever will. It must nevertheless be conceded that such a society does bear at least a passing resemblance to our own – and to Western democracies in general.

In view of the course taken by European history during 1989, perhaps this should not surprise us. For one of the many messages which are inscribed on recent developments in the Soviet Union and Eastern Europe is that our long established democratic perspective on totalitarian states is based upon a false understanding of our own history. For more than a century – and particularly since 1917 – we have consoled ourselves with the fiction that totalitarianism is what happens when democracies collapse. Recent events in the Soviet Union, in Poland, in East Germany, in Czechoslovakia and in Romania suggest that the reverse is true: democracy is what happens when totalitarian regimes collapse. For it is in the nature of totalitarian regimes that they do not collapse 'outwards' into unrestrained liberty. They tend, rather, to collapse 'inwards' into a state of authoritarian democracy, which can be maintained precisely because the restraints and disciplines of totalitarianism have already been deeply internalised during long periods of terror, tyranny and cruelty.

If we were more familiar with our own history this pattern would not be so surprising. For, as I have tried to emphasise in this essay, our own history is deeply marked by cruelty and repression, and by the use of religious terror as a means of enforcing social and ideological conformity. That is why we should pause before celebrating the 'freedom' we now enjoy. For to a very large extent the history of that freedom is a history of internalised repression.

In this respect the battle which has taken place over *The Satanic Verses* is itself very revealing. In theory – in the theory, that is, of the liberal intellectuals who are most involved in the controversy – the battle is one between rigidity and religious authoritarianism on the one side and tolerance, flexibility and democratic freedom on the other. The question which must be asked, however, is whether that theory will stand up if we test it against the reality of what has actually happened in the year since Khomeini's death-threat. I do not believe that it will. Moreover, I believe that the more searchingly the question is asked, the more we are likely to find that the account which I have already given of our own conscience-centred 'cultural revolution' can be used to throw a disquieting light on the affair in general and on the ethos of liberalism in particular.

In the first place it must be conceded that Rushdie affair has occasioned a great deal of authoritarianism as well as much rigidity and intolerance. Anyone who ever doubted that great religions have been among the most significant cultural begetters of authoritarianism, and that they can encourage others to behave with cruel and murderous rigidity, should by now have had their doubts laid to rest by the way in which the most extreme Islamic fundamentalists – and above all the Ayatollah Khomeini himself – have reacted to the publication of *The Satanic Verses*. But it would be quite wrong to suggest that Islam has been alone in displaying rigidity and intolerance. One of the earliest campaigners against *The Satanic Verses*, Dr Hesham El-Essawy, first voiced his objections to the book shortly after it was published in September 1988. As chairman of the Islamic Society for Religious Tolerance, he was subsequently invited by the BBC to take part in a debate with Salman Rushdie about *The Satanic Verses*. The debate took place on January 30th 1989, some two weeks before the Ayatollah pronounced his death-sentence on Rushdie. Shortly after Khomeini's threat Dr El-Essawy wrote to Rushdie again. In his open letter, which *The Guardian* described as 'most friendly and respectful', he recalled their earlier meeting:

> It is not very easy for me in a place of relative freedom to write to you in your place of relative captivity, but I must. You will remember that on our train journey back from the BBC debate in Birmingham on January 30, I went to you, extending my hand in peace and asking you to bring this matter to an end by agreeing to a simple erratum for historical and factual mistakes. You refused, saying: 'You want me to apologise. I will never apologise. I said what I said and will never stand down.'
>
>   The half-apology that you later offered was quickly accepted by this society and myself as a full one.... Unfortunately by then it wasn't my acceptance that mattered.... I do not think that it will make you happy to stay where you are and watch people die. I

do not think you will be happy to see a crisis of an unprecedented nature.

Your fellow writers, who are supporting you to the last drop of their ink, are making it much more difficult for you to make a brave move. They seem to be driving you into a position of enforced martyrdom. For them, freedom of expression has become a fetish. To them that alone is sacred, but if this crisis has proved anything to us it is the fact that it will never do to divorce what you say from your freedom to say it. Both you and the Imam Khomeini have demonstrated that very adequately. Please do not be tempted to indulge their cause – first take good care of your own.

As the holder of the copyright to *The Satanic Verses* please put an end to all the suffering. Instruct your publishers here and abroad to stop publishing.

The letter is significant in a number of respects. What is perhaps most interesting is the privileged access it gives us to a meeting which took place well before Khomeini pronounced his death-threat. In this meeting the request for 'a simple erratum' which is put to Salman Rushdie seems, with hindsight, a mild and reasonable one. Its mildness should not betray us into thinking that it is made gently. For behind it there is evidently the same kind of iron resolution which has been shown by many Muslims throughout the affair – a rigid determination to preserve the sanctity of the Koran against all insult. But the rigidity is by no means all on one side. For Rushdie's response is very far from being accommodating or flexible. He does not simply refuse the specific request, he refuses in the most general terms to consider any form of compromise or apology.

In the circumstances such seeming intransigence on Salman Rushdie's part is perhaps not surprising. For we must bear in mind that, even before the Ayatollah Khomeini issued his death threat, the storm of opposition which had met *The Satanic Verses*, both in India and in the Muslim communities of Britain, had already placed Rushdie in a uniquely terrible position. Under this kind of stress most people tend to react by clinging desperately to any ideological certainties they may possess and may well behave with a degree of rigidity that is unusual.

Rushdie's own reaction, then, is not difficult to understand. What is much more difficult to accept is the manner in which some people offered him the support which he needed so badly at the time. For some did this not unconditionally but in such a way that it became almost obligatory for him to maintain the rigidity of his initial response.

This tendency, which is noted by Dr El-Essawy in the words I have quoted above, can be seen clearly in a contribution to the debate made by the author of an editorial which appeared in *The Observer*. The editorial appeared on February 19th, the day after Rushdie had responded to Iranian demands for an apology by issuing a statement profoundly regretting 'the distress that publication has caused to sincere followers of Islam'. *The Observer* argued that 'neither Britain nor the author has anything to apologise *for*'.

> Both can, as Rushdie has done, regret the offence caused or the anger stirred, but not the act itself. For the right to perform that act, to create and publish a book, has been fought for too painfully to be tossed aside in the desire for a quieter life. Those who ask that it should be are forgetting their own history – from Socrates to Stalin. Galileo is admired for his intellectual courage, not his retractions before the Inquisition.
>
> In this light the British Government's response has been cautious and late...
>
> The harsh lesson of the past – a lesson thousands of people have died to defend – is that it never pays to compromise... In the end, Mr Rushdie must have the right to publish his book and the freedom and security to publicise it. He is entitled to nothing less.

It is interesting that a few days later, writing in *The Guardian* on the same issue, Michael Foot drew a very different lesson from history. He suggested that the lesson of the past was that endless bloodshed could be avoided only when each side learnt that it must be ready 'to abjure absolute victory...The great persisting threat to our world derives from this pursuit of absolute victory. Once it was Hitler's creed, and once it was Stalin's...' Michael Foot goes on to suggest that the fundamentalist voices who have denounced any move towards détente or rapprochement are 'strident, absurd, or indeed wicked'.

Having started from a premise diametrically opposed to that adopted by *The Observer*, Michael Foot manages to reach, by the end of his article, exactly the same conclusion. There can be no doubt, however, which view of history is the saner of the two on offer. It is most certainly true that there have been moments in history when any compromise would be wrong. Munich was one of them. But this does not change the fact that the entire history of successful international diplomacy has been, very largely, a history of compromise. When compromises have been abjured by both sides on principle, the result has in many cases been war – very often a Holy War. By far the most disturbing feature of the whole Rushdie affair is that, while some of the main Muslim proponents have indeed shown a willingness to compromise – as is apparent from Dr El Essawy's open letter to Rushdie – the most vocal supporters of *The Satanic Verses* have, like the author of *The Observer* editorial, displayed a rigidity which sometimes seems to verge on fanaticism.

As a result the battle over *The Satanic Verses* has at times itself come to resemble a Holy War. On the one hand are zealous Muslims who appear to have made a fetish of their own sacred scriptures, and on the other hand an informal alliance of liberal intellectuals, journalists and writers who seem, as Dr El Essawy himself suggests, to have made a fetish out of their right to free expression, and are prepared to defend the integrity of a novel's text with just as much rigour and literalism as some Muslims show in defending the sanctity of the Koran.

To put the matter in this way is, I believe, to do far more than simply offer an ingenious analogy. For the more closely we examine liberal rhetoric, the more it seems that we are indeed dealing not with a battle between religion and secular liberalism but with a clash between two forms of essentially religious ideology. Indeed, some evidence for this view comes from no other quarter than Salman Rushdie himself, in one of the most interesting of all the contributions which have so far been made to the debate.

On January 22nd 1989, soon after *The Satanic Verses* had been burnt during public demonstrations in Bradford, *The Observer* published an article by Rushdie, in which he reflected on the recent events. In the course of this article he suggests quite directly and unequivocally that for him, at least, the art of the novel has been adopted as a substitute for religious faith – a faith which he is, by implication, prepared to defend with all the zeal shown by the Bradford Muslims in defending their faith:

> Dr Aaadam Aziz, the patriarch in my novel *Midnight's Children*, loses his faith and is left with 'a hole inside him, a vacancy in a vital inner chamber'. I, too, possess the same God-shaped hole. Unable to accept the unarguable absolutes of religion, I have tried

to fill up the hole with literature. The art of the novel is a thing I cherish as dearly as the bookburners of Bradford value their brand of militant Islam... So the battle over *The Satanic Verses* is a clash of faiths, in a way...

How fragile civilisation is; how easily, how merrily a book burns! Inside my novel, its characters seek to become fully human by facing up to the great facts of love, death and (with or without God) the life of the soul. Outside it, the forces of inhumanity are on the march. 'Battle lines are being drawn up in India today,' one of my characters remarks. 'Secular versus religious, the light versus the dark. Better you choose which side you are on.' Now that battle has spread to Britain I can only hope it will not be lost by default. It is time for us to choose.

The notion that the man who loses his religious faith is left with 'a God-shaped hole' inside him is one which would, in all probability, strike very few chords among most religious fundamentalists. For traditional religions have not imagined God as existing in some way 'inside' the human body or the human imagination. But the notion is supremely fitting to our own post-Puritan, largely agnostic culture. For it describes with considerable poetic force the end result of a cultural process in which the external God of the Bible – or of the Koran – is first internalised in order to become a God-within, and subsequently put to death by the stones of the rationalist consciousness.

In this whole violent process, however, the religious consciousness is not extinguished. It is preserved, as it were as a vacuum, whose zealous emptiness yearns to be filled once again with faith. It is into that zealous emptiness, as Rushdie himself confesses, that he has poured the art of the novel, so that the novel has become his religion, the faith which he is prepared to defend against all who challenge it.

His willingness to defend this faith is expressed in the traditional apocalyptic imagery of all the ancient religions. So familiar are we with this imagery and so dull have become our reactions to it, that the enormity of what Rushdie is actually proposing in the last paragraph of his *Observer* article may escape us. We may fail to notice that, like religious leaders of earlier ages, he is actually summoning us to a battle, a Holy War. It is a Holy War to be fought out in terms of the same glib, implacable antitheses which have been encountered in earlier battles, a war between humanity and the forces of inhumanity; between the forces of light and the forces of dark. This, then, is a religious crusade. But it is a religious crusade to end all religious crusades. For this time the forces of light are represented by the the troops of secularism, and the goal of their crusade is nothing other than to put to death religion itself. Nor are we allowed to be bystanders at this battle, however bloody it threatens to become. It is, we are told, time to choose.

Once again it is very difficult to know just how much responsibility Rushdie himself should be required to bear for his own words. For although these words were written before the Ayatollah Khomeini's death-threat, they were still written under very severe pressure indeed and show all the signs of great personal stress. But the words nevertheless remain and the alarming thing is that their rigid crusading zeal has been generally accepted as being entirely compatible with a libertarian philosophy of tolerance and flexibility.

Indeed, if we look away from Rushdie's own response, to the words of some of those who have supported him, we will sometimes find even clearer signs of rigour and religious zeal, combined with hints of intolerance for the sincerely held views of others. 'Who is this man of God,' asked Leon Wieseltier, during the course of an American writers' rally held after Khomeini's death-threat had been issued, 'who has no mercy in his heart? But then let us be his match, and in the defense of Rushdie, in the defense of the imagination, in the defense of the mind, show no mercy ourselves. Let us be dogmatic about tolerance....' The problem with this statement is that it modulates from an entirely justifiable condemnation of Khomeini's death-threat into an acceptance of his example as the model according to which the defence of freedom must be conducted. Once again the shadow of the Crusades falls across the twentieth century, and religious rigidity is met with nothing other than religious rigidity.

This same writers' gathering in New York was addressed by some of the country's best known literary figures, including Susan Sontag, Joan Didion and E. L. Doctorow. But according to one report it was Norman Mailer who seemed to capture the mood of the writers best. The duty of the novelist, said Mailer, was to engage in speculation:

That is what we are here for – to speculate on human possibilities, to engage in those fantasies, cynicisms, satires, criticisms and explorations of human vanity, desire, and courage, that the blank walls of the mighty corporations like to conceal from us. We are scribblers who like to explore what is left to look at in the interstices. Sometimes we make mistakes and injure innocent victims by our words. Sometimes we get lucky and make people with undue worldly power a bit uncomfortable for a short time. Usually we spend our days injuring each other. We are, after all, a fragile resource, an endangered species. It is not untypical of the weak and endangered to chew each other up a little on the way down. But now the Ayatollah Khomeini has offered us an opportunity to regain our frail religion which happens to be faith in the power of words and our willingness to suffer for them. He awakens us to the great rage we feel when our liberty to say what we wish, wise or foolish, kind or cruel, well-advised or ill-advised, is endangered. We discover that yes, maybe we are willing to suffer for our idea. Maybe we are even willing ultimately, to die for the idea that serious literature, in a world of dwindling certainties and choked-up ecologies, is the absolute we must defend.

Mailer's words have an undeniable power. In them once again we are brought face to face with the fundamentally religious consciousness of the modern novelist. Indeed, what Mailer pronounces is nothing other than a creed. It is a creed written for a church whose members are so individualistic, so locked into their own creative consciousnesses that they rarely meet. But it is a creed which, given all the usual agnostic qualifications, they mostly share, and which, given the provocation of a seeming Antichrist who is most certainly a heathen, they are prepared, silently, to recite together. What is perhaps most alarming is that, in this creed, literature, which might best be seen as providing a haven from the vast and relentless absolutes of religion, has suddenly itself become a vast absolute, whose perfection and sanctity must be defended against all those who threaten it.

Yet again the shadow of the Crusades falls across the twentieth century. And lest we should mistake its outline Mailer was soon reminding both his fellow writers and the world's media of the hugeness of his religious passion. For, if Salman Rushdie were to be killed, he later told a news reporter, we must, each of us, be prepared to step into his shoes and be killed in his place. Only in this way could serious literature be protected, along with that freedom of expression which is the democratic right of all.

Literature, then, was not simply an absolute. It was an absolute which was to be defended in the same way that the most precious absolutes of the West have always been defended – by the creation of a cult of martyrs.

All this religious imagery and passion should make us pause. Nor should we make the mistake of assuming that the imagery is merely fortuitous – that it has simply been improvised hastily from the materials which are nearest to hand. For the story which this imagery tells is one that goes deep into the history of Judaeo-Christian culture. Behind all this imagery, and the unmistakably religious zeal which accompanies it, there is to be found nothing other than that profound internalisation of the religious consciousness which lies at the heart of our own continuing cultural revolution.

For the religion of Norman Mailer is not a distinctively modern religion. It is a religion whose ancestry can be traced back in a direct line to the religion of John Milton, and to Milton's idealisation of the writer's conscience as the ultimate authority on moral questions, an authority more sacred than that of the holy scriptures themselves.

Milton himself, of course, wrote quite unashamedly from within a Christian, Puritan tradition. His *Paradise Lost* was, in one sense, nothing other than a subjective redaction of scripture – a poetic version of his own personal 'Bible-within'. Nor was this kind of literature exceptional. Indeed, the vast majority of English literature of the seventeenth and eighteenth centuries is profoundly Christian not simply by default but by passionate intent. This applies not only to those who were, like Milton or Samuel Richardson, Puritans themselves, but also to a whole host of other writers including the latitudinarian Fielding and the Anglican Swift – whose *Gulliver's Travels* is not, as many assume, an exercise in sceptical agnosticism, but an exposition of the Christian doctrine of Original Sin so impeccably orthodox that it is now completely mysterious to the majority of modern literary critics and, it need hardly be said, to practically all contemporary Anglican divines.

The consciously Christian character of most 'serious' English literature was maintained, more or less, throughout a very large part of the nineteenth century. But the more the novel became established as the main vehicle of the internalised Christian – or Jewish – conscience, and the main seminary of 'internalised theology', the more confidently novelists began to seek to subvert old orthodoxies, to play with the god-like character of the novelist's own fabulous creative powers and to transgress, through their fictional *personae* at least, old moralities.

As our own century has progressed this agnostic, experimental character of the novel has become so pronounced as to be almost tiresome. Not only this, but a restless and shallow critical concentration on the novelist's transgressions has tended to obscure what exactly it is the novelist is seeking to transgress. This is not, ultimately, the tyranny exercised over the imagination by narrative form or structure; it is the much older and narrower tyranny of Judaeo-Christian ideology and morality.

For this was the terrible burdensome clutch of luggage which the Puritan novelist started out with in the eighteenth century, at the beginning of his Pilgrim's Progress. Throughout the eighteenth, nineteenth and twentieth centuries, from the time of Sterne to the time of Joyce and D.H. Lawrence, repeated attempts have been made to unpack this luggage or to throw it overboard altogether. But the attempts have failed and, as the tradition of the novel has become more complex, the moral burdens carried by contemporary novelists have become, if anything, even more weighty and more cumbersome. Whether we look to the novels of Samuel Beckett or William Golding, of Norman Mailer or Philip Roth, of Malcolm Bradbury or Iris Murdoch, of Margaret Atwood or Jeanette Winterson, of Ian McEwan or Salman Rushdie himself, it is almost impossible not to perceive, beneath the playful or erotic or cynical or experimental surface of their fiction, the huge burden of moral earnestness which contemporary novelists continue to carry.

Although the internalised Christian conscience of the eighteenth century Puritan novelist has, in the centuries which have elapsed since, undergone a process of radical secularisation, it remains fundamentally Puritan in its form and is possessed of all the rigour and the implacable literalism which we associate with Puritanism. So long as the faith of contemporary novelists in the redeeming power of serious literature is allowed to develop unchallenged, then this Puritan zeal is almost completely invisible. But if this faith comes under serious attack, or if the sanctity or integrity of its secularised scriptures is threatened, then the seemingly quiescent church recovers its internalised religious wrath and becomes what it has always been – a Church Militant, which is prepared to fight and even to die for its beliefs, and to campaign with implacable defiance for its right to express these beliefs without restriction, however hard and narrow they may be, however much hurt they may cause to the sensitivities of others.

This, I believe, is what has happened over the case of *The Satanic Verses*. For the furore which it has caused is not a simple battle between fundamentalism and freedom. It is a battle between two factions of the same religious tradition – the Judaeo-Christian tradition to which, ultimately, Islam itself belongs. It is a clash not between religious authoritarianism and freedom but between two kinds of rigidity, two forms of fundamentalism.

In this battle what the most extreme liberals are really advocating, whether by intention or by default, is not, after all, any principle of freedom or tolerance. What they are defending ultimately is the right – or the duty – which has always been most sacred to our intolerantly monotheistic religious culture. It is the right to proclaim the superiority of their own revelation, and to abuse the gods who are worshipped by other, supposedly inferior cultures. For since, as I have tried to show, Christian and post-Christian rationalism is itself a profoundly blasphemous religion, impervious because of its own narrow rigour to the blasphemous insults of others, hard-line liberals who campaign for completely unfettered rights to blaspheme are in effect campaigning for the right to offend the members of other cultures by abusing their religion. This, unwrapped from the scrolls of commentary which have already been written on the *Satanic Verses* affair, is the real principle which is at stake. And it really is high time that it was so unwrapped. For we can then decide whether this principle – which is a principle of intolerance – is indeed one we wish to go to war in order to defend.

One of the problems which has faced us throughout this whole controversy is that this substantive issue of doctrine has tended to be concealed behind a secondary debate which concerns the authority of the individual conscience. Because, historically, our culture has sought to extend to the dictates of the individual conscience – and particularly the conscience of artists and intellectuals – the same kind of inviolable sanctity which was originally enjoyed only by the holy scriptures, there has been a tendency to divorce the issue of freedom of expression from any moral question about what is being expressed.

It should be noted that, to the extent to which they take this view, liberal intellectuals are actually transferring to the question of the artist's right to free expression the same kind of rigour and the same blind zeal that the most militant kind of religious fundamentalists bring to the exposition of their own holy scriptures. For the religious fundamentalist does not pause at the end of every verse of the sacred book in order to debate whether God was right or wrong, too lenient or too cruel, or whether a particular injunction should be accepted or rejected. He does not do so because, enjoying as he does the rich luxury of faith, he has long ago been able to pass the painful burden of his moral conscience into the safe-keeping of the God he worships. Having thus entirely surrendered his moral conscience, he is free to defend the sanctity of his holy book with a zeal which is undiminished by any direct responsibility for what it actually says.

Authoritarian liberals, it must be observed, do something very similar. For although they have given up the luxury of faith they have failed to recognise that such loss of faith brings with it the very kind of burdensome moral responsibilities which fundamentalists have fled from throughout the centuries. They have failed to recognise, in other words, that in a godless liberal democracy a novelist's freedom of expression cannot ultimately be divorced from the moral and political implications of what he or she actually says. Instead, liberal intellectuals have gone on applying to the 'bible-within' of the individual conscience, and to the redaction of that bible in the form of the modern novel, exactly the same habit of mind as our Puritan forbears applied to the Bible. Surrendering their own moral conscience to an abstract faith in freedom, they have defended the textual integrity of all novels with the same kind of blind zeal which Puritans once brought to their defence of the scriptures. The proposition that certain portions of a novel are blasphemous and should be retracted enrages these liberals just as much as a proposal to delete certain portions of the gospels would have enraged seventeenth century Puritans, or a request for a ban on certain parts of the Koran would enrage the true followers of Islam.

The hazards of such a position should be clear enough. Indeed this new form of fundamentalism-without-faith is ultimately far more dangerous than any form of religious fundamentalism. Extreme liberals, of course, are not so naive as to agree in advance that they will submit to any laws artists may propose, or even agree with any opinions they may express. But, misquoting Voltaire, liberals frequently do undertake to fight to the death to defend artists' rights to express any opinions they may choose to. The problem with this position, if maintained consistently, is that it leads directly, by unstoppable logic, into a completely amoral universe. It is a universe in which the novelist's right to advocate torture, rape, murder and genocide must be defended just as resolutely and as zealously as the right to advocate liberty and laughter, and to celebrate affection and sexual love.

Liberals have long been aware of this objection to their position and tend to react by shifting uneasily, like a policeman, from one foot of their argument, which advocates absolute freedom of expression, to the other, which advocates merely freedom within the law. They have also shown a tendency, having noisily driven traditional religious faith out of their house through the front-door, to re-admit it silently through the back-door in some secular disguise. They thus frequently attempt to resolve the dubiety of their position by taking refuge in the belief that art is in itself morally good – or at least that it is more good than bad. But a blind faith in the absolute or approximate goodness of art is ultimately no less dangerous than a blind faith in the moral goodness of God. The danger of traditional god-centred faith is precisely that the goodness of God, once established as a moral fact, may be used to justify all manner of cruelty and oppression. Exactly the same danger attaches to any belief in the moral goodness of art. For societies tend to get the kind of artists they deserve, and a cruel and narrow society is likely to breed cruel and narrow artists. Indeed, in our own secularised and agnostic culture the greatest threat to humane values seems increasingly likely to come not from murderous faith, as it has done for many centuries, but from murderous art.

It is because we need to guard against this ever present danger that any tendency to divorce the artist's freedom of expression from what the artist actually says should be resisted.

To take this position does not mean that we should meekly submit to any form of censorship which governments care to impose upon us, or that we should defer automatically to any pressure group or religious group which takes issue with something that a novelist – or anybody else – has said. What it does mean is that we should stop propounding liberal myths and acknowledge quite openly that absolute free speech does not exist, either in this society, or in any other.

In our own society both artistic expression and every other form of public utterance are constrained not only by the rule of law but also by internalised restraints of decency, tact and morality. By their very nature artists will frequently wish to challenge both these forms of restraint. For one of the most vital tasks which faces all artists is not that of defending a vast area of freedom which we already possess. It is that of repossessing the vast areas of the imagination and of society itself which have already been annexed by the forces of repression. Because the human imagination can never be ultimately confined, artists will always be free to join the forces of subversion in order to engage in such raids on the occupied territories of the mind. But with this freedom comes responsibility.

The greatest responsibility which all artists must bear is that of discriminating between those restraints which are narrow, cruel or repressive, and against which the human imagination should rebel, and those restraints which are necessary for the preservation of tolerance and human decency. The great danger for all artists is exactly the same danger which faces those who would engage in political subversion – it is the danger of enrolling in revolutionary causes, or armies of liberation, which, because of the narrow rigour of their own militant ideals, are set upon a course which can only end by strengthening the forces of repression they set out to overthrow. It is against this danger that we should be eternally vigilant. Above all we should never encourage either artists or publishers in the belief that they may escape their civic, moral and political responsibilities simply by waving the flag of 'democracy' or 'free expression'. Perhaps more importantly still, no publishers should ever believe, or be put under pressure to believe, that they have an absolute obligation to publish a particular work simply in order to uphold some abstract 'freedom to publish'. For one of the most precious components of the democratic freedom to publish is the freedom *not* to publish a particular work. In any society where tyrants and torturers press for a platform for their views, this freedom is zealously guarded by those publishers who possess it. Because neither art nor artists are immune from narrowness and cruelty, or from dangerous political misjudgments, we should guard it just as zealously in our own society.

So far as the constraints of the law are concerned, a different set of considerations applies. One of the main purposes of the laws which constrain freedom of expression is to maintain public order. The laws achieve this end by restraining provocative and insulting behaviour, and discouraging those who have legitimate grievances from having recourse to violence by allowing them recourse to the courts.

In the vast majority of cases the existing laws will be sufficient to maintain public order. But it is very important, if we are to uphold the rule of law in this area, that a sufficiency of legislation should be maintained. If any particular civil or social or religious conflict becomes so huge that it begins to threaten public order, or the rule of law itself, then we should always be prepared to consider creating new legislation, or reforming old legislation, in order to resolve or lessen the conflict in question. The response to the publication of *The Satanic Verses* has already posed a serious threat to the rule of law, not least because of the way in which extremist Muslims in this country have frequently repeated in public Khomeini's death threat against Salman Rushdie, without suffering prosecution. They have done so partly, it would seem, because of their deep and passionate conviction that the blasphemy laws of this country are an affront to natural justice. In this respect, at least, they are at one with the majority of liberal intellectuals. For, as the International Committee for the Defence of Salman Rushdie has itself argued, our ancient blasphemy law has no place in a modern, multi-cultural society. The International Committee has, as we have seen, proposed that the blasphemy law should be abolished *without replacement*. I have already explained why I believe that such a move would be wrong, and it seems to me more likely that in the long term we will need, simply in order to maintain the rule of law, new legislation which does protect non-Christian faiths against obscene abuse, or against incitement to religious hatred.

The problem of framing such legislation is a complex one and I do not wish to engage in all the intricacies of the debate here. There is, however, one point which should be made in relation to the pamphlet on blasphemy produced by the International

Committee for the Defence of Salman Rushdie. For although this pamphlet does have some virtues, which I acknowledged in the last chapter, the guide which it offers to recent legal debates on the issue is less than reliable and, in some respects, seriously misleading.

The real character of the pamphlet in this respect can perhaps best be judged from its treatment of the Law Commission Report *Criminal Law: Offences against Religion and Public Worship* (1985). For, having described this report as 'a cogent and wide-ranging summary of the issue', the authors of the document go on to treat it as their central authority, referring back to it repeatedly and quoting from it frequently. What is remarkable, to say the very least, is that nowhere in the entire pamphlet do we find any mention of the most unusual feature of this particular Law Commission Report – namely that the Law Commissioners disagreed amongst themselves. Of the five Commissioners only three endorsed the majority recommendation. The other two put their names to a Note of Dissent. They accepted the defects of the present law but went on to argue that it should be replaced by a more coherent piece of legislation which offered protection not simply to Christianity but to all religions. In making this recommendation it would seem that they were influenced by two arguments which were quoted in the majority report. The first was a submission by an outside working party who suggested that some legal restraints on blasphemy were necessary for the protection of social harmony:

> If scurrilous attacks on religious beliefs go unpunished by law they could embitter strongly held feelings within substantial groups of people, could destroy working relationships between different groups, and where religion and race are intimately bound together could deepen the tensions that already are a disturbing feature in some parts of this country. It is for this reason that our Working Party recommends that the protection of the law must be extended to all religious beliefs.

The report also quoted a similar remark made by Lord Scarman in the House of Lords judgment on the *Gay News* case. Lord Scarman, who is often regarded as the most liberal of British judges, came out in support of extending the current blasphemy laws:

> My Lords, I do not subscribe to the view that the common law offence of blasphemous libel serves no useful purpose in the

modern law. On the contrary, I think there is a case for legislation extending it to protect the religious beliefs and feelings of non-Christians. The offence belongs to a group of criminal offences designed to safeguard the internal tranquillity of the kingdom. In an increasingly plural society such as that of modern Britain it is necessary not only to respect the differing religious beliefs, feelings and practices of all but also to protect them from scurrility, vilification, ridicule and contempt.

Both these points of view were incorporated into the Law Commissioners' Note of Dissent, which proposed the abolition of the offence of blasphemy and its replacement by a new offence based on the recognition that it is 'the duty on all citizens, in our society of different races and of people of different faiths and of no faith, not purposely to insult or outrage the religious feelings of others'.

This disagreement between the Law Commissioners was important not only because it was extremely unusual but also because the Note of Dissent had a significant posterity. For in 1987 the Bishop of London's Working Group on blasphemy made it the basis of its own recommendations to Parliament. At the time at least, this recommendation was fully endorsed by the Archbishop of Canterbury, Dr Runcie, who said that he 'had considered the Bishop's new Report with care' and that he was happy to identify himself 'with its reasoning and conclusions'.

Yet in spite of the obvious relevance of all these facts to the *Satanic Verses* affair, they are passed over in complete silence by the International Committee's pamphlet, which does not even cite the views of Lord Scarman. Through such strategic silences the pamphlet creates the impression of a surge of informed opinion, based on almost complete unanimity among lawyers, which favours total abolition of the blasphemy laws *without replacement*. The International Committee even expresses the view that blasphemy laws should be abolished not only in Britain but also 'in all other countries' and that in Britain 'the law as it stands violates the European Convention on Human Rights'. In this connection, however, the authors of the pamphlet omit another significant fact. For, as Professor Simon Lee has pointed out, in the course of a lively and cogent contribution to the debate to which I am indebted, the disappointed defendants in the *Gay News* trial had themselves taken their case to the European Court of Human Rights in Strasbourg.

This court had dismissed their complaint, declaring that it was 'manifestly ill-founded' and ruling quite explicitly that British law on blasphemy was not in conflict with the European Convention.

The distorted picture created by the International Committee's document has helped to sustain the view that the real disagreement in the current debate is between ageing bishops clinging to the blasphemy laws in an attempt to preserve an archaic past, and modernising secularists or humanists who would do away with any protection for people's religious feelings altogether.

It is no doubt true that there are some who favour retention of the current blasphemy laws on sentimental, conservative or socially retrogressive grounds. But theirs are certainly not the most significant voices in the recent debate. For by far the most important aspect of recent changes in thinking about blasphemy has been the recognition, which would normally be regarded as 'progressive', that we no longer live in a Christian society based upon a single national culture. We have for many years inhabited a plural society made up of many different cultures and faiths. In such a society, with its inevitable racial and cultural tensions, a small but significant number of lawyers, clergymen and laymen, have begun to take the view that some protection of people's religious feelings is necessary not primarily for spiritual or religious reasons, but in the interests of social harmony.

The emergence of this distinctively modern view can be traced back at least as far as the early part of this century. For it was in 1917 that Lord Sumner suggested that the view which maintained that the law of blasphemy protected only the established church was 'a strange *dictum*'. He pointed out that 'After all, to insult a Jew's religion is not less likely to provoke a fight than to insult an episcopalian's...' But it is only in relatively recent years that a more radical position has begun to emerge, which looks forward to the abolition of the old law and its replacement by an entirely new law whose scope is not restricted to Christianity alone. Sometimes those who have proposed such a change have obscured how radical their views are by continuing to use the term 'blasphemy' to describe the new offence which they envisage. This is true not only of Lord Scarman's remarks, which have already been quoted, but also of the Law Commissioners' Note of Dissent and the Bishop of London's report to the Archbishop of Canterbury. Other participants in the debate, such as the lawyers Sebastian Poulter and

Simon Lee, have preferred to drop the term 'blasphemy' from their proposals and talk instead of a new offence based, as in Northern Ireland, on 'incitement to religious hatred'. It was this proposal which received a measure of support from the Archbishop of Canterbury when he shifted his position on the question in an interview reported in *The Guardian* on March 23rd 1990.

We should not allow differences of vocabulary and emphasis, however, to obscure the kinship between the two kinds of proposal. What they have in common above all else is a desire to move away from a theologically inspired framework which once helped to sustain a form of tyranny, towards secular legislation which is designed to protect relatively powerless minorities against oppression or abuse by others.

The debate about legislative reform in this area is still in its early stages and a number of extremely important questions have yet to be resolved. This is partly because, in our largely secular intellectual culture, the whole topic of religious abuse and vilification remains obscure and inaccessible to most observers. What is clearly needed is a great deal more discussion of all the key issues. Otherwise there is a danger of legislating in the dark and of creating new laws which are actually obsolete before they even reach the statute book, or which are intrinsically ineffective.

Partly because of such difficulties it seems clear that any legislative answer to the general problem of religious vilification lies some way in the future. Because of this the problem which faces us now, over the troubled and terrible issue of *The Satanic Verses*, cannot be solved by the law. Perhaps, indeed, like most disputes between neighbours, it will be resolved much more speedily if both sides forget about the possibilities of legal redress, and spend a little more time considering each other's point of view.

Alas we have become, in our Protestantism, more virtuous than the myths which taught us virtue; we judge them barbaric.

John Updike

A conviction that one is writing or speaking on the side of virtue can license an indulgence in fantasies that virtue itself would ordinarily compel one to forswear.

Dan Jacobson

Introduction to the Illustrations

Some tyrannies — Calvin's Geneva, Stalin's Russia, or indeed, Ceausescu's Romania — are both absolute and absolutely unacceptable; in the face of them blasphemous thoughts, which may be both extreme and obscene, are not simply excusable, they may be psychologically necessary in the struggle to preserve the vitality of truth and the possibility of liberation.

But rebels and dissidents who treasure such blasphemies in the secrecy of their imaginations should not make the mistake of treating them as though they are part of a common currency which is acceptable to all. For in the most extreme tyrannies blasphemous thoughts belong only to the black-market economy; they should be traded and exchanged, if they are traded and exchanged at all, only furtively and only with extremely discretion. For if any coin of this forbidden currency is pressed by mistake into the hand of a member of the secret police, or a member of the Securitate, then it is likely that the reprisals will be swift and cruel. Rebels and dissidents should not simply avoid this fate for their own good, they should avoid it for the common good. For the resources of freedom are not infinite, and those who carelessly squander them will amost certainly diminish the possibilities of liberation.

In this necessary furtiveness is concealed the most destructive of all the features of rigid, authoritarian regimes. For the more effective any tyrannical regime becomes at the task of policing the blasphemous utterances of its citizens, and the nearer it comes to the tyrant's ideal of suppressing blasphemy altogether, the more likely it is that the blasphemous thoughts which cannot be uttered will become a dark burdensome secret in the consciousness of those who are tyrannised. Whenever *this* happens, the great danger is that blasphemous impulses which cannot be expressed publicly are redirected so that they are vented not against the absolute and tyrannical state, whose authority the blasphemer ultimately resents, but against real or imaginary secondary tyrannies, which supposedly threaten the stability of this state.

"Down the throats of some they violently
thrust knotted clouts, and then with a string
pulled them up again, whereby they displaced
their bowels" — Clarke (1651). The judges
supervise the torture and the scribe takes down
the prisoners confession.

The clearest historical examples of displaced blasphemy are perhaps those
provided by the Christian church in Europe during the time the Inquisition was
at its most powerful. One of the effects of the Inquisition's rise to power was that
blasphemy and heresy, which had always been rigorously condemned by
Christian orthodoxy, were now cruelly suppressed. Yet, far from destroying the
impulse towards blasphemy, the very cruelty and rigidity of the Inquisition
seems to have redoubled unconscious resentment not simply against the
Inquisitors themselves but against the rigour and narrowness of the rule of
Christ, whose perfect agents they claimed to be. The extremity and obscenity of
the blasphemous impulses which resulted can perhaps best be judged by
considering the collective fantasies which were elaborated at this time around
'witches'.

A witch. Sixteenth-century drawing
by Niklaus Manuel Deutsch.

These witches, who in reality did not exist at all, became, in effect, the unacknowledged *alter-egos* of devout Christians, expressing their unconscious resentment against Christianity, and their most obscene and blasphemous impulses. They were imagined not simply as the Devil's worshippers, but also as the Devil's emissaries, agents in a diabolical conspiracy to spread evil and contagion into the farthest corners of Christendom.

It was this vision which was, for some two hundred years, expounded, elaborated, documented or illustrated by some of the most pious and educated minds in Europe. It was by such minds as these, working in a troubled alliance with the popular imagination, and including the Inquisitors themselves, that the idea of witchcraft as an unclean, anti-Christian conspiracy was created and subjected to a wholly fantastic elaboration.

The witches sabbat as illustrated by Pierre de Lancre (Paris, 1613)

According to some contemporary accounts the sabbat — after feasting and a central ritual involving incest, sodomy and copulation with demons — would customarily conclude with the Devil sending witches back to their homes to redouble their crusade of evil against Christendom, after first having endowed them with the power, knowledge and potions to do this. He would also instruct them to ensure that, when they next took communion, they retained the sacred host in their mouths so that they might afterwards spit it out on the ground in contempt of the body of Jesus. Sometimes such ritual abuse of the host supposedly took place at the sabbat itself, where witches would spit, trample or urinate on both the host and the cross.

The witches sabbat. Title page of a German
book on witchcraft, Leipzig, 1668.

The Devil in the form of a goat is enthroned in the centre. He receives the
obscene kiss from one of his followers, while other witches dance naked with
demons. In the foreground a demon excretes into a chamber-pot. The open
tankard positioned nearby suggests that the demon's excrement will later be used
as a eucharistic host, administered in obscene contempt of the Christian
sacrament.

74

Judensau, fifteenth-century woodcut.

The kind of displaced blasphemy which is encountered in the European witch-craze, far from constituting an abnormal, aberrant or unprecedented episode in Western history, shows the Judaeo-Christian imagination working in one of its most characteristic ways. The same unconscious resentment against Christianity was often discharged by blaspheming not against Christianity itself but against rival faiths. In Christian anti-semitism two slightly different forms of psychological displacement can often be seen at work simultaneously. On the one hand it would appear that Christian anti-semites unconsciously identified with the Jews whom they accused of all kinds of blasphemies against Christ — including the torture or desecration of the host. On the other hand, they were able simultaneously to satisfy blasphemous impulses by transforming their unconscious hostility towards Christianity into extreme and sometimes obscene attacks on the sacredness of Judaism.

The popularity of the *Judensau* motif derived from its obscenity and from the way it harnessed Christian misogyny. By vividly associating Jews with an animal which was both dirty and female, and showing them sucking greedily at its udders, or preparing to lick its anus, the motif suggested that Jews were the eternal unclean children of God, who were to be identified with the sow they clung to; supposedly unable to wean themselves away from the realm of sin, pollution and 'womanly' carnality into pure 'manliness', they were to be seen as bearers of the stench and the female 'uncleanness' of their sow-mother.

RABINI SCHEMHA
MPHORAS

RABINI, SCHEMHAMPHORAS,

These sixteenth century engravings are all based on the Wittenberg *Judensau*, a sculpture in Martin Luther's church at Wittenberg which Luther himself made famous. In his *Von den Juden*, Luther condemned all Jews as greedy and maggoty: 'You are unworthy to look at the outside of the Bible, let alone read inside it. You should read only the Bible which is under the sow's tail and gobble and guzzle the epistles which fall from there.' Subsequently Luther identified the sow with the Talmud. This interpretation was taken over by another Christian polemicist who went on to accuse Jews of impiety and of blaspheming against Christ. See Chapter One.

Christian bestiary, twelfth century.

Der Stürmer, 1934.

The representation of the sinner as an unclean 'child' suckling on the udders of a sow was a part of Christian iconography for at least six centuries. In many cases the sinners were identified specifically with Jews. In the twentieth century the motif was taken over by National Socialist propaganda. The caricature in *Der Stürmer* is headed 'Literary History'. The pig is labelled 'Jewish publishing house'. Beneath it were the words: 'When the sow dies the litter perishes too.'

ADORATVR PAPA DEVS TERRENVS.

Bapſt hat dem reich Chriſti gethon/
Wie man hie handelt ſeine Kron.
Machts jr zweifeltig ſpricht der geiſt/*Apoc.18.*
Schenckt getroſt ein/Gott iſt ewers heiſt.
                Mart. Luther D.

HIC OSCVLA PEDIBVS PAPAE
FIGVNTVR.

Nicht Bapſt/nicht ſchreck vns mit deim
Vnd ſey nicht ſo zorniger Man. Bann/
Wir thun ſonſt ein Gegenwehre/
Vnd zeigen dirs Bel vedere.
                Mart. Luther D.

The same pattern of fantasy, in which blasphemous impulses are projected and displaced, can also be discerned in the anti-Catholic fantasies of Puritanism. The Lutheran Reformation in Germany was itself brought about in the medium of anti-semitic and anti-Catholic propaganda whose obscenity would eventually be surpassed only by the fantasies of Hitler and Streicher. One of the most effective techniques of Luther's supporters was to use woodcuts — the earliest form of mass propaganda — in which the sanctity and holiness of the Roman Catholic church was subjected to systematic sexual and scatological abuse. In this way, the Lutheran church was able to establish its own authoritarian regime and its own hold on the popular imagination by actually encouraging extreme and obscene blasphemy and redirecting it against the ideological enemy — the Roman Catholic church.

In these two woodcuts crude obscenity is used to preach the cause of spiritual refinement. On the left a German mercenary soldier excretes into the papal tiara while two others adjust their dress after having done the same. The crossed papal keys on the shield beneath have been replaced by a pair of thieves' jemmies. The Latin title reads 'The pope is adored as an earthly God.' The inscription claims that the pope has treated the kingdom of Christ as the pope's crown is treated here. On the right two peasants bare their buttocks in order to fart at the pope, who is holding out a bull of condemnation, identified by the hell-flames which spring from it. The German text mocks the pope for attempting to intimidate people with his bull while the Latin inscription satirises the custom of kissing the pope's foot in reverence as a sign of subjection, suggesting that the lips of the anus would be more appropriate for this custom than the lips of the mouth.
[Source: R. W. Scribner, *For the Sake of Simple Folk*, CUP, 1981]

78

Throughout the history of the Church devout Christians have tended to project all manner of libidinous or cruel fantasies onto the apocalyptic beast of Revelation, which was imagined as an incarnation of blasphemy. (See cover illustration). The seven-headed beast was sometimes portrayed being ridden by the Whore of Babylon who carried a golden cup filled with 'the wine of fornication' which she had used to make the inhabitants of the earth drunk. Here Dürer has prettified and bowdlerised the cruelly misogynistic vision of John's apocalypse.

The enemies of Christendom, including both Jews and Muslims, were frequently equated with the apocalyptic beast. In 1213 Pope Innocent III described Muhammad as 'the Beast of the Apocalypse'. In subsequent centuries the view of Islam as a demonic force, and of Muhammad himself as Antichrist, became deeply established in the Christian imagination.

In this sixteenth century Lutheran woodcut Christ is shown trampling triumphantly upon a three-headed version of the apocalyptic beast. One of the heads is that of the Pope who spews out monks and demonic spirits. The second head is that of the Devil disguised as an angel. The third is that of a Muslim — specifically of the Turk who was seen at the time as a sign of the last days and as identical with Gog and Magog, the hosts of Satan who figure in Revelation 20.7.

Similar apocalyptic imagery may be found either in an overt or a covert form in the propaganda of nearly every repressive and authoritarian social movement. In the seventeenth-century engraving reproduced above, which projects a massive fantasy of male domination, the place of Jesus has been taken by Oliver Cromwell, who is shown standing in triumph on the dead body of the Whore of Babylon and the reptilian form of the seven-headed beast — the Roman Catholic Church.

It is to the stern patriarchal tradition of Puritans like Cromwell and John Milton that our modern doctrines of liberty of conscience and freedom of speech belong. Frequently, like the original Puritan theories of freedom, these doctrines secrete illiberalism and intolerance.

In the European witch hunt, in Christian anti-semitic fantasies and in anti-Catholic propaganda, we encounter a supremely effective, and almost entirely unconscious strategy of social control. Through this strategy a repressive, authoritarian ideology maintains or establishes power by deflecting the blasphemous resentment to which it gives rise onto a real or imaginary secondary tyranny.

We may well like to believe that our own society has outgrown such essentially religious patterns of control. But one of the most disturbing features of the *Satanic Verses* debate is that, at the heart of this whole affair, and in spite of Salman Rushdie's own intentions, a similar process appears to be taking place.

Partly because of the dispute, Islam is now in danger of becoming the most important of all the West's modern apocalyptic enemies, and of filling the vacancy left by the sudden 'conversion' of the 'evil empire' of the Soviet Union. For even in our secular culture the old demonological perception of Islam has survived, and has indeed been greatly strengthened. Some liberal intellectuals seem to be intent on translating the vision of Pope Innocent III into modern terms. For, by daring to suggest that blasphemy should be outlawed, Muslims have themselves blasphemed against one of the sacred doctrines of Western intellectuals. As a result Islam has once again found itself treated, at times at least, as though it were the very incarnation of blasphemy, the Beast of the Apocalypse, which must be subjugated in a Holy War of words fought this time not by Christian crusaders, but by crusading unbelievers.

One of the most significant effects of this confrontation has been to deflect criticism away from the rigid and insensitive orthodoxies of our own political culture, and redirect at least some of this resentment against an external enemy. Few intellectual causes this century have succeeded so well in protecting Western forms of economic and cultural imperialism by what wartime atrocity-propagandists would refer to as 'a strategy of compensation'.

The dangers of such political and cultural scapegoating should not be underestimated. They are particularly acute because Islam is itself an apocalyptic faith and, in its most extreme manifestations, has responded to its own demonisation by demonising the West. In Iran, for example, America has for many years been commonly portrayed as 'the Great Satan'. The second part of this book explores some of the dangers associated with this clash of intolerances.

Part Two

CHAPTER THREE

'In Good Faith'

As the date of the first anniversary of the *fatwa* approached it became clear that there was going to be a renewal of interest in the Rushdie affair on the part of journalists. What most people were not prepared for, however, was the extraordinary scale of the media coverage which eventually developed.

This coverage had in fact started in the middle of January to coincide with the first anniversary of the book burning in Bradford. The debate was effectively initiated on Friday January 12th by *The Guardian*'s highly regarded political columnist, Hugo Young. A year previously Young, like most political liberals, had been forthright in his condemnation of Khomeini's *fatwa* and in defending Rushdie's freedom of expression. At the time, he had not shown any great sympathy for British Muslims or any insight into their distress. A year later it was clear that he had considered the whole issue more deeply, and that he was also possessed of the moral courage to shift his ground in order to take account of the complexities of what has become, perhaps, the most difficult of all free-speech issues:

> In the coolness which is afforded by the passage of time...certain reasonably objective facts associated with *The Satanic Verses* are pretty clear, and bear on the debate about the paperback. One would think that the author himself, at any rate, would be bound to consider and re-consider them, in the fastness to which his work has confined him.
>
> It is, for example, quite clear that the quality of Muslim outrage and distress is not to be measured only by the barbarous threats of Rushdie's would-be assassins. It has a graver dimension in the minds of people who unfailingly observe the law but who were cut to the quick by the obscene and sardonic way this book dealt with another book, the *Koran*, which they regard with a most unwestern seriousness. How supremely important it should be for an author to drive home these insults, irrespective of any of their consequences, is at least a question which deserves discussion.

Young went on to recall that eighteen people had been killed during rioting over the book and that a hundred people had also been injured. While stressing that it would be wrong to deduce that Rushdie had caused these casualties, he suggested that 'if one were the author whose work was the proximate pretext for such terrible events, one might feel obliged to think about them with a certain awed humility before re-opening the contest'.

At no point in his article, however, did Young show any signs of agnosticism about the value of free speech. He argued instead that the debate was no longer about free speech since Rushdie's work was 'now in print to the extent of far more than a million copies'. This being so, an alternative did present itself:

> ...which is for the author, humbled by what he has wrought and satisfied that his freedom of speech remains unimpaired, voluntarily to renounce the paperback, on the deeply considered grounds that it could do more harm than good.
>
> This would not be a ban. It would surrender subsidiary but not essential rights. It would be done by the author and not by his publisher. It would in no way concede the Muslim case that the book should never have been written. It would be the magnanimous gesture of an author with a million copies already on the market, who, looking at his situation in the round, asked himself quite how entitled he was to insist on risking other lives than his own, for the sake of a principle which in this case has long since ceased to be imperilled. Is it possible for an author, without endangering his freedom by one iota, to contemplate that there might be matters which on occasion balance it? The paperback *Verses* looks like one such moment.

Hugo Young's article immediately gave rise to a fierce debate in the correspondence columns of the paper, with opinions sharply divided between those who supported a compromise on the paperback and those who opposed it at all costs. The debate was further fuelled by a full page feature published by *The Guardian* on January 15th. In addition to a telephone interview with Salman Rushdie, the feature included three short articles on the question of whether *The Satanic Verses* should be published in paperback. Nadine Gordimer and Louis Baum argued that it should, while John Le Carré rejected the argument for a paperback on the grounds that the bloodshed it might lead to could not be justified.

The debate which began in *The Guardian* was continued elsewhere – in *The Times*, in *The Observer*, in *The Sunday Times* and in *The Daily Telegraph* where Anthony Burgess set forth his views. But it was in the recently launched *Independent on Sunday* that the issue received the fullest coverage.

The second issue of *The Independent on Sunday* was, indeed, in terms of its content, one of the most unusual editions of a British newspaper which has ever appeared. Almost the entire front page was given over to an interview with Salman Rushdie under the heading 'Rushdie breaks his silence'. The front page also carried an editorial in which the editor declared that, in taking up the issue of *The Satanic Verses*, his newspaper was 'not seeking to reopen old wounds; on the contrary, we hope to open a new dialogue. We shall not only welcome replies from those who disagree with Rushdie, we shall solicit them. They will be printed with due prominence next week.' The editorial concluded with these words: 'The last year has been full of fear and anger. We have all learned a little more about ourselves. It is now time to let reason and gentleness prevail.'

Inside the paper Salman Rushdie was given one of the most powerful platforms ever allowed to any writer, his 7,000 word essay 'In Good Faith' being spread over three full pages. Over the next few weeks, although this essay was rarely examined in any detail, it was widely referred to. A number of writers heralded it as one of the greatest pieces of literary polemic ever written. Others were more sceptical and sometimes their scepticism was both fierce and passionate, as in the case of Michael Dummett, whose open letter to Salman Rushdie was published by *The Independent on Sunday* the following week.

So far as the tone of 'In Good Faith' is concerned, there can be no doubt at all that it was very different from the angry and uncompromising note which Rushdie had sounded in his last piece on the subject in *The Observer* almost exactly a year earlier. Muslims were no longer dismissed simply as agents of darkness. But although Salman Rushdie's tone had changed outwardly, and seemed on the surface conciliatory and even friendly, a close reading of the essay made it clear that his underlying position had changed very little.

In the opening section of his essay Rushdie presents his novel as one which sets out to subvert repressive orthodoxies. 'Throughout human history,' he writes, 'the apostles of purity, those who have claimed to possess a total explanation, have wrought havoc among mere mixed up human beings.' This claim is in itself a persuasive one. For whether we look to the cruelty of the Inquisition, the murderous anti-semitism of Martin Luther, the tyrannical regime which Calvin established at Geneva, or, more recently, to Stalin's Russia, or Hitler's Germany, we will find that in each case cruelty has been sustained by an ideology of absolute purity. It is in the name of purity, God and absolute goodness, or in the name of a rigid, pure and utopian state, that millions of men and women have been murdered.

What is even more disturbing for those of us who were brought up in the West, is that the Christian church itself has been the chief disseminator of absolutist ideologies of purity. Even National Socialism was, whether we like to acknowledge it or not, an ideology which grew up in the heart of Christian Europe. Deeply internalised into its secularist doctrines were Christian ideals of purity together with a long tradition of religious anti-semitism which had been nurtured by the Christian church throughout many centuries.

If Rushdie's novel were indeed a book which radically questioned Western ideologies of purity and power, and if it really did seek to subvert, not by blasphemy, but with all the tenderness, passion, affection and power of the human imagination, the tyrannies of the Judaeo-Christian tradition – of which Islam itself is ultimately a part – then the only reasonable response would be to welcome it. But the novel itself is engaged in no such enterprise. Again and again, as we have already seen, it seeks to subvert ideologies of purity in general by re-imagining, sometimes in blasphemous terms, some of the most sacred traditions of a particular ideology – Islam. And what Rushdie seems not to have understood is that when blasphemy is used in this way, there can be nothing liberating about it. For this is exactly the way in which blasphemy tends to be used by orthodox religious thinkers in order to sustain their own repressive ideologies of purity against the challenges posed by other cultures.

Not only does Rushdie show no awareness of this aspect of history, but it is clear from his essay that, even after a year, he is still quite unable to face up to the huge and disastrous political consequences which had flowed from the publication of *The Satanic Verses*.

The extent and seriousness of these consequences is not really in dispute, for the essay is itself introduced by an editorial statement which reads as follows: 'The publication of *The Satanic Verses* has had disastrous consequences: riots, deaths, enforced isolation for the author, intimidation of the publishers, a deep sense of injury in the Muslim community worldwide. But has the novel simply been misread and misunderstood? Salman Rushdie believes that it has, and proposes "a way forward through mutual recognition of mutual pain".' Once again, the tone of these words is conciliatory. But the underlying message is harsher. For we are in effect asked to believe that neither the author nor the publishers of *The Satanic Verses* bear any responsibility for what has happened since the novel has been published. The people who are to blame for a seemingly endless series of tragedies are Muslims – some of them uneducated, but some of them academically well qualified and highly sophisticated readers of fiction – who have supposedly 'misread and misunderstood' Rushdie's novel.

By far the most surprising aspect of this argument is the manner in which Rushdie evinces a seemingly complete and unquestioning faith in the reliability of artists' intentions as a guide to the work of art they have produced. 'Never trust the artist, trust the tale', wrote D.H. Lawrence. Salman Rushdie, however, disregards both Lawrence's advice and almost the entire history of twentieth-century literary criticism, which has tended to treat artists' conscious intentions with scepticism and to seek out levels of meaning which are unconscious or unintended. In place of this sophisticated critical approach, Rushdie suddenly rediscovers a naive faith in the conscious intentions of the artist and appears to believe that if he proclaims his own holy intentions loudly enough, the unholy results of the publication of *The Satanic Verses* will be annihilated, or neutralised.

The bewildering naivety of this view, and of the authoritarian model of fiction which it implies, is not made to seem any less bewildering by the specific arguments which are advanced in the essay. In seeking to dispose of the accusation that his novel contains 'insults and abuse', Rushdie presents it as a work of dissent:

> What does the novel dissent from? Certainly not from people's right to faith, though I have none. It dissents most clearly from imposed orthodoxies *of all types*, from the view that the world is clearly This and not That. It dissents from the end of debate, of

dispute, of dissent. Hindu communalist sectarianism, the kind of
Sikh terrorism that blows up planes, the fatuousness of Christian
creationism are dissented from as well as the narrower definitions
of Islam. But such dissent is a long way from 'insults and abuse'.
I do not believe that most of the Muslims I know would have any
trouble with it.

This view of the novel as a work of dissent has in fact had a
considerable currency throughout the debate and it has sometimes
led to the charge that Muslim campaigners against the book are
seeking to suppress all criticism of their faith – that, in the words
of a letter published by *The Guardian*, they are campaigning for 'the
absolute right to advocate religious belief without being criticised by
unbelievers'.

Of course there are those within Islam, just as there are in all
religions, who do not like criticism and seek to suppress it. But the
view that the *Satanic Verses* affair is about the suppression of
intellectual debate, or of reasoned dissent, is based on a reluctance
to attend closely to the actual terms of the Muslim protest. For most
Muslims have gone out of their way to distinguish between criticism
and abuse, and to make it clear that they are campaigning only
against the latter and against the use of obscene and violent
language in relation to their religious tradition. In his essay Rushdie
goes some way towards acknowledging this:

> What [Muslims] have trouble with are statements like these:
> 'Rushdie calls the Prophet Muhammad a homosexual', 'Rushdie
> says that Prophet Muhammad asked God for permission to
> fornicate with every woman in the world', 'Rushdie says the
> Prophet's wives are whores', 'Rushdie calls the Prophet a devil's
> name', 'Rushdie calls the Companions of the Prophet scum and
> bums', 'Rushdie says that the whole Qur'an was the Devil's work'.
> And so forth.

But Rushdie's own rather crude parody of the arguments which
have been advanced against his novel is open to objection on a
number of counts. In the first place it is simply not true, as his
words imply, that all those who oppose his novel are unfamiliar
with the conventions of fiction, and that they cannot distinguish
between the novelist and the novelist's characters. What is even
more important, however, is that in the process of ventriloquising
Muslim complaints, Rushdie has actually changed their nature.
What Muslims object to most is not that 'Rushdie calls the

Companions of the Prophet scum and bums', but that a character in his novel refers to them as 'trinity of scum' and 'fucking clowns'. If his novel did indeed portray Muhammad as asking for permission to 'fornicate' with every woman in the world, it would be much less offensive to Muslims than it actually is. In translating these various affronts to Islam out of the obscene vernacular of the novel and into a register which conforms to the proprieties of a Sunday newspaper, Rushdie has actually succeeded in bowdlerising his own book. It is perhaps no wonder that the gelded fiction which results sometimes really does begin to appear quite inoffensive.

By misrepresenting his own novel in this way, Salman Rushdie himself ends by doing precisely what he accuses his Muslim critics of doing. He discusses a book which simply does not exist. The real book, 'not the piece of blubber, but the whole wretched whale', as Rushdie puts it, certainly does encompass all the complexities, the doubtings and the re-imaginings which he stresses in his essay. For *The Satanic Verses* is a complex and highly wrought work of art. But the same real book also contains a great deal of obscene, wounding and contemptuous language and imagery which is used in relation to some of the most sacred traditions surrounding the Prophet Muhammad. At one point in his essay Rushdie does obliquely concede the obscenity of some of his language. But he seems quite unable to understand the offensiveness of this language.

If we read *The Satanic Verses* in the context of Salman Rushdie's other work, it would seem quite clear that one of the reasons he has recourse to obscenity so frequently in the novel is that he genuinely believes that such language belongs to a programme of liberation. Malise Ruthven quotes a passage from the earlier novel, *Shame*, in which Rushdie makes his own attitude towards right-wing Islamic fundamentalism quite explicit:

> So-called Islamic 'fundamentalism' does not spring, in Pakistan, from the people. It is imposed on them from above. Autocratic regimes find it useful to espouse the rhetoric of faith, because the people respect that language, are reluctant to oppose it. That is how religions shore up dictators; by encircling them with words of power, words which the people are reluctant to see discredited, disenfranchised, mocked.

One of the implications of this passage is that any programme which seeks to liberate 'the people' from domination should include an assault on the sacred language of faith in an attempt to 'disenfranchise' the 'words of power'. It is to just such a programme of liberation that the obscenity of *The Satanic Verses* appears to belong. When it is enacted in the novel, however, what this programme reveals is not any genuine libertarian impulse, but rather Salman Rushdie's own inability to discriminate between the different ways in which obscenity can be used.

Obscenity can be both precious and liberating, and we should recognise this a good deal more than we do. But when obscenity is used to grease the dagger of insult, it becomes one of the most dangerous of all imaginative weapons. We should have no doubt that the obscene language in *The Satanic Verses* is directed against the hard shell of rigidity and intolerance which is so visibly a part of Islamic fundamentalism. But that is not how ordinary Muslims experience this language. They experience it as a dagger thrust deep into the affectionate heart of their faith – the most precious of all their possessions.

As an artist Salman Rushdie might be expected to be alert to such feelings of hurt. His evident insensitivity in this regard, however, is not simply his own fault. It is *our* fault for creating a culture which, in its entirely understandable desire to liberate the sexual imagination from taboos, has frequently failed to grasp the amount of destructive violence which has been locked up in the realm of the obscene. In this respect it might well be observed that we have as a culture devoted a great deal more time and energy to fighting for the right of novelists to use the words 'fuck' and 'cunt' than we have ever given to considering the psychology which is implicit in our usage of these words, and in the enormous power which they possess.

In the context of a trusting relationship both words can be the focus of some of the most precious human feelings; it is because of their affective richness, and the emotional wealth which has been locked into their obscenity, that any culture which values emotional vitality should always resist those who seek to ban these words either from literature or from life.

But even within a sexual relationship these obscenities are fraught with a dangerous ambivalence. They can all too easily cease to belong to the rhetoric of liberation and become part instead of a rhetoric of power, dominance and subjugation. Indeed, it would seem that the further these obscenities are removed from a context of trust and emotional intimacy, the more likely it is that they will be used as vehicles not of emotional richness but of hatred and contempt. In its most common and everyday usage the word 'fuck' is one of the hardest and most violent words in the English language; more often than not it is used in a way that implies the existence of a hated Other who must be punished, subjugated or suppressed. The identity of this hated Other becomes clear when we consider that, according to the most basic psychological grammar, whatever exceptions there may be to it, women are the idealised or degraded objects of the word. For it expresses, perhaps better than any other single word, the misogyny of our culture, a misogyny so ordinary and so deep that for the most part we do not even recognise that it exists. As Germaine Greer wrote in *The Female Eunuch*, even sophisticated men 'still say "Fuck you" as a venomous insult; they still find *cunt* the most degrading epithet outside the dictionary.' The contents of the Oxford English Dictionary may have changed since these words were written in 1970. But the general truth which they express remains unaltered.

It is such extreme language, which is potentially the most violent and the most insulting of all the registers available to Western writers, which, in the pages of *The Satanic Verses*, is brought into conjunction with some of the most sacred traditions of Islam. Although there are other perceived insults in the book, this in itself would be enough to create a sense of outrage among the Muslim faithful. When it is joined to the brothel scenes where the whores take the names of the Prophet's wives, to the knowing use the book makes of the street obscenities of Bombay and to the use of the ancient Christian term of abuse, Mahound, for Muhammad, it is little wonder that many Muslims have come to regard Rushdie not simply as an opponent of Islam, but as a cultural traitor who has sold some of their most sensitive secrets into the hands of the enemy.

The belated defence which he offers against such charges in his essay 'In Good Faith' is clearly put forward with sincerity, yet it is not any more persuasive for this. He points out, as sympathetic commentators had done before him, that his use of the Christian demonological term 'Mahound' for Muhammad is itself intended to be part of a programme of liberation and he quotes the explanation given in his novel: 'To turn insults into strengths, whigs, tories, Blacks all chose to wear with pride the names they were given in scorn; likewise our mountain-climbing, prophet-motivated solitary is to be the medieval baby-frightener, the Devil's synonym: Mahound.' What is remarkable in itself is that Rushdie should have the insensitivity to repeat, in this particular context, his own bad and tasteless sub-Joycean pun, 'prophet-motivated'. What is far more important, however, is his evident failure to recognise that any programme designed to reclaim language from one's opponents is itself fraught with dangers. It may well be true that some Afro-Caribbeans have chosen to wear with pride the word 'black', but as Muhammad Aslam Qureshi has observed, 'they did it themselves'. For Rushdie, having confirmed that he is not himself a Muslim, to argue that he is reclaiming language on behalf of all Muslims is an act of quite extraordinary presumption.

Even if we disregard such intrusiveness, Rushdie's argument fails to convince. As Malise Ruthven has pointed out, blacks have not attempted to reclaim and wear with pride the word 'nigger'. For some words are freighted with a contempt which cannot easily be unloaded, and to seek to appropriate them would actually be a way of internalising contempt. It may well be true that, with frightening insensitivity, Mrs Thatcher once made some play with the image of herself as the 'Iron Lady'. But does Salman Rushdie really imagine that, having read *The Satanic Verses*, she will soon be referring to herself with pride as 'Mrs Torture'? One of Rushdie's conscious motives for reviving the term Mahound is quite clear. But conscious motives are not everything and simply because contempt clings to the word 'Mahound' as it clings to the word 'nigger' it is difficult to avoid the conclusion that, in spite of all brave intentions, Salman Rushdie is offering to Muslim readers not a renewed sense of pride and dignity but an oblique and unintended invitation to internalise centuries of Christian contempt.

This invitation has, thankfully, been rejected even by some of Rushdie's most highly educated and most westernised Muslim readers. It has been rejected, along with the obscene language which the book applies to Muhammad and his companions, not simply with a sense of hurt but with deep feelings of violation. Once again one might expect that Rushdie, as an artist and a novelist, would be sensitive to such feelings. Over the past year he has certainly experienced feelings of violation himself, feelings which he describes in one of the most memorable and arresting passages of his essay 'In Good Faith'. 'Even if I were to concede (and I do not concede it),' he writes, 'that what I did in *The Satanic Verses* was the literary equivalent of flaunting oneself shamelessly before the eyes of aroused men, is that really a justification for being, so to speak, gang-banged? Is any provocation a justification for rape?'

The point is an entirely legitimate one, and I for one would never dream of questioning the authenticity of the feelings which Salman Rushdie expresses in these words. It is because the punishment to which he has been subjected far exceeds the provocation which he has offered, and because one man is being punished for what is in reality the act of an entire culture – the publication and the critical empowering of a novel – that he is at the moment the victim of a cruel injustice. That being so it is right and just that he should have been given so much support over the past year.

All this having been said, however, it is still difficult to understand Rushdie's own apparent inability to grasp that the feelings of violation which he has experienced over the past year correspond closely to the sense of violation which has been felt by the Muslim community as a direct result of the publication of his novel. Some of the most significant Muslim responses in this respect are discussed by Malise Ruthven in his book *A Satanic Affair*:

> 'We Muslims are a tolerant people but we cannot bear insult.' Such was the gist of several conversations I had with Muslims about *The Satanic Verses* both before and after Khomeini issued his notorious *fatwa*. Even Dr Zaki Badawi, head of the Muslim College in Ealing and one of Britain's most liberal Muslim leaders, felt deeply pained by the book: 'What he has written is far worse to Muslims than if he had raped one's own daughter,' he told *The Guardian*. 'Muslims seek Mohammed as an ideal on whom to fashion our lives and conduct, and the prophet is internalised into every Muslim heart. It's like a knife being dug into you – or being raped yourself.' The Tanzanian scholar Dr Ali Mazrui told an audience at Cornell University that his Pakistani friends had likened the book to a kind of child abuse in reverse: 'It's as if Rushdie had composed a brilliant poem about the private parts of his parents, and then gone to the market place to recite that poem to the applause of strangers...'

This sexual imagery should not be treated lightly any more than should the similar imagery which is used by Rushdie in his essay. For what it helps to do is to locate the obscenities of *The Satanic*

Verses in a human context and to convey one educated and sensitive
Muslim's feeling that in the novel Islam is the victim not simply of
criticism or satire but of an act of cultural rape. If this is so it must
be suggested that it is the victim not so much of Rushdie himself,
as of the Western values which he has appropriated so eagerly. In
the novel the sensitivities of Islam, and its own right to cultural
self-determination are callously disregarded. They are disregarded
in the name of a sophisticated, rationalist and secularist culture
which, as the culture of the West has always done, seems to believe
it has a divine right to dominate, to subjugate, and to claim as its
own imperial property even the most unwilling of brides.

In his essay in *The Independent on Sunday*, however, Salman
Rushdie seeks to present himself not as a cultural imperialist but as
a cultural liberator. It is, it would seem, in this self-appointed role
that he uses the space provided for him by the paper to mount
attacks on a number of opponents. Although he claims in his essay
that he will always 'dissent from the end of debate, of dispute, of
dissent', what is remarkable about these specific confrontations is
his evident reluctance to face up to the detailed arguments of those
who disagree with him. While some opponents, such as the
formidable Dr Ali Mazrui, are ignored altogether, others fall to his
polemical sword, which he wields more in the manner of a saint
slaying the dragons of dissent than of an intellectual engaging in
real debate. Taking advantage of some errors of judgment made by
Keith Vaz over the issue, he ruthlessly attacks him for changing his
position, without ever pausing to inquire into the reasons for this
change. Having disposed of Keith Vaz, he goes on to discuss the
contributions to the debate made by Hugo Young:

> Twelve months ago, *The Guardian*'s esteemed columnist, Hugo
> Young, teetered on the edge of racism when he told all British
> Muslims that if they didn't like the way things were in Britain,
> they could always leave ('if not Dagenham, why not Tehran?');
> now this same Mr Young prefers to lay the blame for the
> controversy at my door. (I have after all fewer battalions at my
> disposal.) No doubt Mr Young would now be relieved if I went
> back where I came from.

What is notable about these words is Rushdie's refusal to engage
with the terms of Hugo Young's argument. Instead of this, he
accuses Young of flirting with racism while failing to acknowledge
that he came so close to racism only because of the unqualified

fervour with which he supported Salman Rushdie's own right to free speech. Having been chastised for the rash terms in which he initially offered his support, Hugo Young is then chastised again for reconsidering his position. Instead of recognising the complexity of Young's latest statement, Rushdie reductively parodies it. Instead of seeking to rebut its arguments he prefers to cast crude aspersions on the integrity of its author and to suggest, without any grounds whatsoever, that Young has succumbed to intimidation and that he harbours racist feelings about Rushdie himself.

In this instance a crude form of character-assassination is resorted to as a substitute for debate. Something very similar happens to another writer who had dared to criticise Rushdie, Rana Kabbani. Kabbani's first book, *Europe's Myths of Orient*, was published in 1986 to considerable acclaim. Among the most significant of the voices which welcomed it was that of Salman Rushdie himself, who described it as 'an important, fierce and judicious book...a wholly convincing analysis of the conscious creation, by Western literary travellers, of an almost completely fictional East, and of the enduring and largely pernicious power of this fiction'. In her *Letter to Christendom* Kabbani maintains the position she had outlined in her earlier book and criticises Salman Rushdie for taking over Western forms of orientalist prejudice against Islam. In 'In Good Faith', however, instead of dealing with her arguments, Salman Rushdie dismisses her contribution in a sentence: 'Rana Kabbani announced with perfect Stalinist fervour that writers should be "accountable" to the community'. On the basis of the single word 'accountable', torn brutally from the context of her entire book, Kabbani thus stands condemned as a Stalinist. The charge has a particularly ironic resonance in view of the fact that, not very long ago, Martin Amis suggested that we needed to raise the issue of 'the accountability of the author in fiction'. Since these words had been quoted by Feroza Jussawalla in an essay published in a special *Satanic Verses* issue of the American journal *Public Culture*, it seems almost certain that Rushdie was aware of them. But while Rana Kabbani is condemned for 'Stalinist fervour', Martin Amis, an enthusiastic supporter of Salman Rushdie, is allowed to use the same word with impunity.

Having dealt with both Hugo Young and Rana Kabbani in this rather unpleasant manner, Rushdie goes on to make an entirely reasonable complaint about what he describes as the 'brutalisation of public debate' in the wake of the *fatwa*. This complaint, however, immediately modulates into another attack, mounted this time on a rather shadowy group of mostly nameless critics:

> And slowly, slowly, a point of view grew up, and was given voice by mountebanks and bishops, fundamentalists and John Le Carré, which held that *I knew exactly what I was doing*. I must have known what would happen; therefore I did it on purpose, to profit by the notoriety that would result. This accusation is, today, in fairly wide circulation, and so I must defend myself against it, too...

Like everything else in the essay, these words should be read with great care. Rushdie begins by making a rhetorical brace of 'mountebanks' and 'bishops' in order to fire a volley of abuse in the general direction of the Church of England. When he goes on to add 'fundamentalists' and John Le Carré to his targets and to italicise the words 'I knew exactly what I was doing' it might well be assumed that he is either quoting or accurately paraphrasing the views of Le Carré. In fact, however, the extraordinary accusation that Rushdie knew 'exactly' what he was doing was actually made by Roald Dahl in a letter published in *The Times* on February 28th 1989. And it was Roald Dahl who went on to imply in the same letter that Rushdie 'did it on purpose' in order to profit from the notoriety which would result.

When John Le Carré expressed his views on the question in *The Guardian* on January 15th 1990 he at no point suggested, or even came near to suggesting, that Rushdie 'did it on purpose to profit by the notoriety which would result'. He certainly implied that Rushdie possessed the kind of knowledge which might have led him to be more prudent; but he made this suggestion in entirely reasonable terms:

> Rushdie is a victim, but in my book no hero. I am sorry for him and I respect his courage, but I don't understand him. In the first place, anybody who is familiar with Muslims, even if he has not the advantage of Rushdie's background, knows that, even among the most relaxed, you make light of the Book at your peril....
>
> I am also unclear about the extent to which Rushdie, perhaps inadvertently, provoked his own misfortune. His open letter to the Indian Government seemed to me to be of an almost colonialist arrogance...

As in the case of Hugo Young, however, Rushdie declines to engage with the actual terms of John Le Carré's criticism. Instead he resorts to a common debating trick. He takes the most extreme and the most easily rebutted of all the charges which have been levelled against him and, failing to attribute it to its real author, Roald Dahl, he puts Dahl's words into the mouth of John Le Carré, who actually said something significantly different, and into the mouths of various unnamed 'bishops', 'fundamentalists' and 'mountebanks'. Having thus crudely caricatured his opposition, he goes on to devote some twelve paragraphs of his essay to rebutting a charge which some fundamentalists have made, but which neither Le Carré nor any bishop has levelled against him. His rebuttal is forceful and persuasive but his victory is empty. For it is the victory of a heavyweight boxer who, fearing defeat, has conjured a shadow into the ring in place of his real opponent and who subsequently takes almost absurd satisfaction in dealing to this shadow a knock-out blow.

Having rebutted the charge that when he wrote his novel 'he knew exactly what he was doing' Rushdie goes on to suggest that the controversy over *The Satanic Verses* should be understood 'as a political event, not a purely theological one'. He argues that in India, in South Africa, in Pakistan and Iran, calls for the banning of his book were part of a powerplay designed to strengthen the hand of the various political factions involved. There is clearly a great deal of truth in this view so far as Iran is concerned. But in the case of South Africa and India, Salman Rushdie's understanding of the political dilemmas posed by his book is open to question. In India by far the strongest argument for banning the book was that only in this way could the threat of extensive communal rioting be avoided. Rushdie, however, has consistently refused to accept the view of many seasoned observers of Indian politics that religion in India is a powder-keg and should be treated accordingly. After he had accused Rajiv Gandhi of seeking to build a repressive society, the *Times of India* made the following reply:

> No, dear Rushdie, we do not wish to build a repressive India. On the contrary, we are doing our best to build a liberal India, where we can all breathe freely. But in order to build such an India, we have to preserve the India that exists. That may not be a pretty India, but it is the only India we have.

In order to maintain his own position Rushdie has been forced to disregard not only these words but also the words of the Nobel Prize-winning Nigerian writer Wole Soyinka who has himself been imprisoned for opposing dictatorship. Soyinka commented in the summer of 1989 that he quite understood the action of the Indian government in banning the book and that 'given India's harrowing situation of religious unrest, I would probably have done the same if I were the Prime Minister'.

In some other respects the argument which Rushdie advances in 'In Good Faith' about the political exploitation of the *Satanic Verses* affair is a great deal more soundly based. He is clearly on much firmer ground, for example, when he suggests that in Britain, the affair has had the effect of swinging the balance of power in the Muslim community away from secular organisations and 'back towards the mosques'. As Malise Ruthven writes in his *A Satanic Affair*, in the short term at least, 'activist or fundamentalist hands have been greatly strengthened by the furore over the book's publication, particularly in the United Kingdom. Before the Rushdie Affair very few people took Dr Siddiqui seriously; now he has a considerable following among British Muslims for expressing a hard-line Khomeinist view.'

Yet what Salman Rushdie is evidently quite unable to face up to, in this essay as elsewhere, is the crucial role which he himself has played in precipitating the entire affair and in provoking at least a part of the Muslim response. At the same time he has been quite unable to grasp one of the most important principles of religious psychology, namely that blasphemy is itself frequently an authoritarian mode of protest, and that those who use blasphemy against religious tyrants will almost always succeed, against all their professed intentions, in strengthening the hand of those tyrants.

Instead of taking some measure of responsibility for even the smallest part of the response to his book, Rushdie takes refuge in the power of assertion. For his answer to any criticism of his own role is presented without any argument at all in an italicised sentence which stands at the head of one of the concluding paragraphs of his essay: '*The responsibility for violence lies with those who perpetrate it.*'

This view is delivered with such an air of finality, that the timid reader, and even the less timid reader, is inclined to submit to Rushdie's assertive power without question. Yet this sentence, perhaps more than any other in Rushdie's essay, *should* be questioned. Does the responsibility for violence *always* rest with those who perpetrate it? When Britain declared war on Germany in 1939 and when British soldiers killed German soldiers in the battles which followed, were *they* responsible for their violence? When forty gypsies turned upon their German guards in the ante-chamber of the Auschwitz gas-chambers and clawed at their eyes with their bare hands, were *they* responsible for their violence? When a woman, after suffering years of abuse, humiliation and mental cruelty from a husband who has never laid a finger on her, finally cracks under the strain and beats him senseless to the floor, is *she* responsible for her violence?

In one sense it is quite clear that the answer to all these questions must be yes. Those who perpetrate violence *are* responsible for their actions. But at the same time it is clear that in these cases, as in countless others, the perpetrators of violence are not *purely* responsible for the violence which they commit. For in a very large number of cases, whatever the legal situation may be, the moral responsibility for violence is divided between those who perpetrate it and those who provoke it. Yet, rather than admit this possibility, Rushdie prefers to escape all responsibility for his own actions by taking refuge in a kind of political slogan-making: 'The responsibility for violence lies with those who perpetrate it.'

Throughout the essay this primary argument is supplemented, as I have already observed, by the loud professions which he makes concerning his own benign artistic intentions. In some cases these professions are entirely persuasive. There is certainly no doubt in my mind that Rushdie's intentions in writing *The Satanic Verses* were, in some sense, holy. But throughout the whole history of religion holy intentions have again and again produced unholy results and have led to war, hatred and conflict. Unable to understand the profoundly apocalyptic nature of his own secularist vision, it would seem that Rushdie is unable to confront the possibility that his own holy and idealistic intentions might mask just as much destructive authoritarianism as the holy intentions of the religious zealots he criticises.

Yet, if we attend closely enough to Salman Rushdie's actual words, it is just this disturbing possibility which emerges. Towards the close of his essay he implies that his own novel and his own political aspirations should be interpreted in the light of recent events in Eastern Europe:

> A great wave of freedom has been washing over the world. Those who resist it – in China, in Romania – find themselves bathed in blood. I should like to ask Muslims – the great mass of ordinary, decent, fair-minded Muslims to whom I have imagined myself to be speaking for most of this piece – to choose to ride the wave; to renounce blood; not to make Muslim leaders seem less tolerant than they are. *The Satanic Verses* is a serious work, written from a non-believer's point of view. Let believers accept that and let it be.

These are extraordinary words not least because they reveal Rushdie's capacity for self-deception about the nature of his audience. His essay is quite clearly composed for the benefit of, and only accessible to, a tiny intellectual elite. Yet he is still able calmly to express the belief that he is addressing 'the great mass of ordinary...Muslims'. Such blindness to one's own membership of a narrow elite is in itself remarkable. What is even more disturbing is the manner in which, in one of those glib antitheses we have encountered before, Rushdie goes on to offer Muslims a stark and simple choice: either they should accept *The Satanic Verses* and cease to campaign against it, or, because of history's implacable march towards freedom, they will find themselves bathed in blood. It is difficult to understand from Rushdie's words whose blood this will be. But it is also extremely difficult not to read his words as an oblique and ominous threat – a secularist, apocalyptic threat made in the name of freedom against those who, because they seek to defend their religious faith against what they experience as intolerable insults, are now implicitly defined as the enemies of freedom.

If Salman Rushdie's words had been written twenty years ago it would have been relatively easy to dismiss them as the rhetoric of a mere writer. But in the past two or three years writers have come a great deal closer to real political power than has been the case for a long time. That Rushdie is acutely aware of this was made clear in the interview with Blake Morrison which appeared on the same day as his essay. Contrasting recent developments in Eastern Europe with the events of 1968, Rushdie suggested that this time there had been a real shift of power:

And what's optimistic about it is that those in power seem intelligent and restrained: it's rather heartening to find that when people take over political control they're far more reasonable than politicians.

To have a serious writer like Vaclav Havel running a country, quite possibly two serious writers running countries if Vargas Llosa wins the election in Peru, is a sign that perhaps the world is a less hopeless place than I thought it was. *It would be nice if it happened here.* (my stress)

What is perhaps most significant about these words is the ease with which Rushdie shifts from the notion of 'people' taking over from politicians to the notion of 'writers' running a country. It would appear that in his own political imagination there is no real distinction between 'people' and 'serious writers'. Writers are now apparently to be understood as the ideal embodiment of the people, just as Marxist intellectuals were once understood as the ideal embodiment of the proletariat.

It is perhaps in relation to just such political assumptions that we should view Rushdie's essay and, in particular, the stark choice he appears to offer Muslims. From this perspective it is not at all clear that democratic government by the literary intelligentsia would, were it ever to be instituted, be any less cruel than the dictatorship of the proletariat once was. This is not, it should immediately be said, because members of the literary intelligentsia are themselves disposed to commit acts of cruelty or physical violence against their political opponents. Far from it. It is because most literary intellectuals of the post-war generation have been so conditioned by intellectual pacifism, and have become so alienated from their own violent impulses that they can no longer understand the violence of others. Locked into a universe of rational and intellectual discourse which is remote from real feelings and real violence, they have at the same time ceased to understand the internalised violence of the political world which we have ourselves created. Most importantly of all, they have not understood the ease with which, given the right social and economic conditions and the wrong intellectual and moral response on their part, this internalised violence can be converted into real political, religious or racial violence of the kind we now believe can happen only in Belfast, in Beirut or in Jerusalem.

CHAPTER FOUR

Towards the Anniversary

In view of the weakness of its central arguments, Salman Rushdie's essay 'In Good Faith' seemed to invite a critical and sceptical response. There are good reasons to suppose that his essay was indeed received sceptically in many quarters. But this was not the impression given by reports which were published in the press at the time. The day after his essay was published, *The Independent* carried a news story under the headline 'Writers welcome Rushdie's defence of *Satanic Verses*'. The story was apparently based on telephone interviews conducted with four writers, one politician, one rabbi, one Asian academic and one Muslim politician. Of these eight people, four were critical of Rushdie to some degree. The story began, however, by reporting that Rushdie's essay had been 'warmly received by fellow writers yesterday'. It went on to report that 'many praised his reasonable tone, but some also expressed concern that his arguments might fall on deaf ears'. The report quoted the comments of Arnold Wesker, who described the essay as 'reasoned and reasonable', and Penelope Lively, who said that she found the essay 'dignified and moving'. Michael Foot was even more enthusiastic, saying: 'It's the most brilliant piece of political writing I've read in my life. It could change the whole future of this controversy if people read it.' Michael Ignatieff said: 'In 50 or 60 years' time, this essay will be regarded as one of the great classic defences of the novelist's art in this country. It's that important.'

Although this story was published as a news report and was therefore supposedly impartial, the presentation of the report was clearly biased. Not only this but the chorus of approval which it reported for Rushdie's essay had every appearance of having been orchestrated, by the simple expedient of inviting reactions to Rushdie's essay primarily from writers who had already declared their support for *The Satanic Verses*.

In spite of this evident bias it could not be said that the coverage given to the issue by *The Independent* was one-sided. The same edition of the paper printed two brief but thoughtful replies to Salman Rushdie's essay written by two of the most acute Muslim commentators on the affair, Tariq Modood of the University of Swansea and Shabbir Akhtar of the Bradford Council of Mosques. The next week, true to its word, *The Independent on Sunday* published a number of brief articles commissioned from those who disagreed with Rushdie's essay as well as several letters from Muslims who objected to his point of view. There was no comparison between the prominence and space given to these letters and the front page treatment accorded to Rushdie. But newspapers, unlike public service broadcasters, are under no obligation to maintain 'balance', nor should they be put under pressure to do so. Since it is probably true that, during the week which followed the publication of 'In Good Faith', *The Independent* and *The Independent on Sunday* gave more space to the Muslim point of view than any other British newspapers have ever done, they should be given full credit for this.

There are, however, a number of questions which might be asked about other aspects of *The Independent on Sunday*'s coverage of the issue. Indeed, if responsible journalism is valued at all in this country, these questions need to be asked as a matter of urgency.

One of the most important questions concerns not what the paper did write about the issue but what it did not write. For one of the striking omissions from the huge coverage it gave to the whole subject was any attempt to exercise some of the most basic and valuable of journalistic skills – the skills of the trained reporter. In this respect *The Independent on Sunday*'s daily counterpart, *The Independent*, acquitted itself much better. For on January 6th 1990 it published a full page feature on the issue including a thoughtful report from Bradford by Jack O'Sullivan, which stressed the heterogeneous nature of Islam and the reluctance of liberal intellectuals to concede this. Even Jack O'Sullivan's article, however, did not explore in detail the complexities of life in Bradford under the shadow of the Rushdie affair.

A full month later, *The Independent on Sunday* did not even attempt this task. For during this crucial period the issue was treated as though it were primarily an intellectual or literary question concerned with abstract principles and ideals. Nobody, it would seem, wished to offend the sacred principles of intellectuals by actually sending a real journalist into one of the communities most affected by the Rushdie affair, in order to talk to the ordinary men, women and children who had to live with its consequences. Indeed, while it was clear that *The Independent on Sunday*, like most newspapers, could draw on the services of correspondents in all manner of far-flung places – in Tokyo and New York, in Jerusalem and Johannesburg, in Berlin, Bucharest, and Beirut, it would seem that it had no correspondent in Bradford.

At least one other newspaper was not defeated by this problem. *The Observer* came up with the imaginative solution of sending its Beirut correspondent, Julie Flint, to Bradford. The article which she wrote was published on the front page of the Review section on February 11th, 1990.

Sensitive, probing and judicious, always alert to small significant details, her reporter's eye captured a reality which had escaped many more lofty commentaries. For her piece was a model of its kind, an immensely valuable example of an undervalued art – the art of journalism. Because I believe that it provides a much needed perspective on the entire issue, I will quote from it at length:

> 'Nadeen woz 'ere,' say the graffiti outside the front door of 68 Southfield Square, one of Bradford's forty mosques. Inside, in a large front room drenched with air freshener, a pint-sized child in a Batman T-shirt is reciting his prayers. On the other side of the city, the office of the Young Muslims looks more like the Boy Scouts, with photographs of the summer camp and a hand-written sign saying: 'Tuck Shop'.
>
> It is now a year since Ayatollah Khomeini issued his *fatwa* decreeing death for Salman Rushdie. Bradford, which opened the campaign against *The Satanic Verses* in Britain, is firmly established in the popular imagination as a citadel of Muslim radicalism, a hotbed of agitation by adherents of a cruel and intolerant faith. As a result many non-Muslims feel remarkably free to be abusive. 'Scum of the earth', says a local taxi-driver. 'We've given them too much. Now they expect it and want more.'
>
> But reality does not fit the image and it comes as a surprise to find that the now-famous Council for Mosques is a draughty, run-down place heated by a one-bar fire and that only one of the forty mosques is purpose-built. The remainder are unused church halls, unwanted and unlovely warehouses, and crudely converted terraced houses conspicuously lacking in petrodollars.

Julie Flint went on to relate how the Council of Mosques was still the subject of almost daily abuse following its decision to burn a copy of *The Satanic Verses*, and because of reports that two of its members had endorsed the Ayatollah's *fatwa*. 'The fact that one of the two has since been forced out of the council and that the second claims that he was misquoted has changed nothing: the first impression remains.' The publication of *The Satanic Verses* and the *fatwa* had led the Muslim community in Bradford into a vicious circle of prejudice and persecution. In the decade that preceded the affair, not a window had been broken in the Council of Mosques. In the last year, however, the building had been attacked at least four times. Sher Azam, the conciliatory president of the Council of Mosques, was still surprised by the amount of hate mail which poured into it. Earlier, his young daughter had received telephone calls saying, 'We will burn your house down and cut your throats.' Azam comforted her by saying that the people who were going to cut her father's throat were not going to tell her first. He installed an answering machine and now will not allow his family to pick up the phone when he is not there.

This threat was only one of the many which have been received by prominent Muslims in the city. Mohammed Ajeeb, a former Lord Mayor of Bradford, had received abusive letters saying: 'What you deserve is the gas chambers'. The racialism which walked Bradford's streets was not new. Julie Flint recalls that in 1979 the Commission for Racial Equality issued a damning indictment of Bradford's race relations policies. Throughout the next ten years the situation, however, had steadily improved. One of the great tragedies of the Rushdie affair is that, as Julie Flint herself puts it, 'it has undone much of the good work of the Eighties'.

'Rushdie' has joined the lexicon of classroom slang. White children shout it on the streets and scrawl it in the underpasses: 'Salman Rushdie is our hero...Rushdie rules'. Asian youngsters are stopped on the street and asked: 'Have you seen Salman Rushdie? If you did, would you kill him?' 'Rushdie, Rushdie' is a popular chant when Bradford city play away from home.

It was this kind of taunt that lit the fuse of the worst rioting seen in Bradford since the *fatwa*, rioting that was purely racial in character. It began in the predominantly Asian West Bowling district, an open ghetto on the edge of the all-white Holme Wood estate where police have recently mounted cameras on tower blocks in an attempt to crack down on thuggery.

Mamoor Khan, a 21-year-old Asian, was one of the first victims. 'Me and my mates were just walking up here and there were six or seven lads walking down. As we got to them they started chanting this Rushdie stuff – "Salman Rushdie is our leader". We walked past them and they started shouting "You black so-and-sos". The next minute I heard some footsteps and thought: "Oh no!" One of the guys pulled a knife on me. I was watching him – not bothering about his other mates – and I got ear-whacked from the side with a bar. They had lasses there and all and one of them took her shoes off and whacked me on the head with her stilettos.'

The following weekend a group of 30-40 whites armed with sticks invaded West Bowling, 'booting anyone who was in the way and smashing windows'. Word had leaked out from the local pub that trouble was planned and West Bowling had alerted the police.

'They said, "Don't worry, right? We've got it under control, right?"' says Khan. 'We thought "fair enough, we'll leave it to them". But there wasn't one copper on the street when they came. It took them 35 minutes to get here. By then there were loads of our lads out and everyone started throwing bricks at them. The white guys must have been having their dinner by then, home in bed.'

After that fiasco West Bowling took the law into its own hands. Scores of young Asians smashed pubs and beat up white youngsters every weekend until police simply cut the area off. The battle lines were clear-cut: black against white.

'I've seen plenty of white lads being attacked,' says Khan. 'But you can't say nowt because they'll think you're one of them. Those months were really bad. Racism was inside them. Salman Rushdie just brought it out. If they hate blacks why don't they say so rather than making excuses about Rushdie? If white guys walk past you now, your eyes are on them all the time. They've done it before. You can't trust them.'

The impression given by the article was that, without the need for any segregation statutes, a new form of racial separation seemed to be growing up in the city, and, as Julie Flint's report made clear, it was related to the *Satanic Verses* affair:

Although many expected far greater trouble in Bradford, it is clear that race relations, already interacting with industrial decline, have been severely damaged.

In West Bowling a new community centre is used by blacks from Friday to Sunday and by whites from Monday to Thursday.

'Your best friend was against you,' says Mamoor Khan. 'Now you see him, but that's that. You don't speak. Before Rushdie we used to go to a white kid's house in the evenings to watch videos. But he had windows smashed and moved out of West Bowling. Now its just Pakis and a few West Indians.' Builders working on a new mosque are unable to find white architects: 'They want nothing to do with Muslims.' Local papers are accused of refusing to print letters from Muslims. 'We'll start our own paper,' says Mohammed Sadeq, founder of the Bradford-based Muslim Youth Group of Great Britain. 'We don't have to depend on the white man.'

Bradford's Asians are tolerant about everything except the 'religious pornography' of *The Satanic Verses*. Mamoor Khan is adamant about this: 'The guy is sick. I can't go and write a book about the Queen, can I? I'm not religious, but that book really hurt me. If it came down to dying for it, I would...'

...If *The Satanic Verses* comes out in paperback it seems virtually certain that these tensions will explode into violence. 'The longer we prolong the issue, the greater the anger will be in the community,' says Ishtiaq Ahmed. 'Other communities blow hot and cold. But when the most patient community blows up and goes outside the law, it'll be very sad and unfortunate.' Tim Whitfield, of the Council for Community Relations, is more specific: 'As long as the paperback doesn't come out, anger will continue to dissipate but will be squeezed into other outlets like single-sex schools. If the paperback comes out, there will be demonstrations and a lot of anger. There is fear that the frustration which has built up will move into terrorist type activity. It only needs one or two fanatics.'

Julie Flint's article was one of the most disturbing reports on a British city to have appeared in a newspaper for a very long time. There can be no doubt that it did not reflect all the complexities of a many-sided conflict. But by eschewing remote intellectual arguments, and focusing instead on events and feelings in one of the communities most affected by the affair, it struck at the roots of some of the most sacred beliefs of our society – above all the intellectual's comfortably abstract, armchair-faith in free speech. Perhaps because her piece threatened this belief so deeply, and because it could be discounted as the work of a 'reporter', it seemed to make curiously little impact at the time. But her article remains and it disturbs still, not least because it establishes that some kind of connection, however complex and remote, really did exist between the publication of a post-Modernist novel in September 1988 and the action of a white teenage girl in Bradford who, not very long ago, removed her stilettos and started to beat a Muslim youth over the head with them. The article also posed disturbing questions about the way that *The Satanic Verses*, and its reception and defence by liberal intellectuals, had seemed to give a kind of moral licence to racism which had always been latent. 'Those months were really bad. Racism was inside them. Salman Rushdie just brought it out.' Mamoor Khan's account of what happened is clearly an oversimplification of a very complex process, which involves in its chain of connections not simply an individual but an entire literary and intellectual culture. But that such a chain of connections, linking literature to racialism, really did exist would now be difficult to deny.

Julie Flint's report, however, appearing as it did on 11th February 1990, was too late to influence one of the crucial stages of a debate which had already been raging for more than a year. For *The Independent on Sunday*'s huge coverage of the issue had begun the previous week and it included not only Rushdie's 7,000 word essay but also a full page feature under the title 'Should the paperback version be published?' Though it might well be thought that people like Mamoor Khan and Tim Whitfield of the Bradford Council for Community Relations were ideally qualified to answer this question, they were not consulted. For the feature was based not on the views of those living in communities which would be directly affected, but on answers to a letter sent to 'over 100 leading authors, publishers, booksellers, politicians and opinion-makers'. The letter invited those contacted to answer the question 'Should *The Satanic Verses* be published in paperback?' and permitted them to add a brief statement. Of the replies which were printed, a substantial majority were in favour of the paperback.

The impression which was conveyed by the feature was of a surge of informed opinion, particularly strong among politicians and authors, in favour of publishing the book in paperback. 'The chief opponents to paperback publication were', we were told, 'members of the Muslim community and booksellers'. What was perhaps most remarkable about the entire feature was that, although the letter sent out to contributors appeared merely to be inviting material for a journalistic feature, the answers given by individuals were now treated as though they were part of a ballot.

Readers of *The Independent on Sunday* were solemnly told that 'the *poll* came down exactly three to one in favour of paperback publication going ahead'. In the strangest twist of all, two contributors were referred to as having 'spoilt their ballot papers'.

If the paper had indeed conducted a poll on this issue then it must be said that it had done so without informing those whose votes were eventually counted. Its method of opinion-sampling was also unusual. Of the thirty people whose views were quoted in the feature, some twenty-five or more had already declared their views on the *Satanic Verses* affair in public. Of the writers whose statements were printed, many had already emerged as being among Salman Rushdie's strongest supporters, including Ian McEwan, Kazuo Ishiguro, Martin Amis, Tariq Ali and Hanif Kureishi. All three of the American writers quoted – Arthur Miller, Norman Mailer and Susan Sontag – had already given public backing to Salman Rushdie's book and the same was true of the only three politicians whose views were quoted – Michael Foot, Paddy Ashdown and Roy Jenkins. The statements of those who opposed the paperback were no less predictable. Of the eight people who answered 'no', seven had already expressed negative views about *The Satanic Verses* in print. Indeed, among all the statements published, perhaps the only unpredictable response came from James Kirkup, the poet who had been at the centre of the *Gay News* blasphemy trial in 1977. While declaring his opposition to all forms of censorship, Kirkup wrote that he did not believe 'it would be wise or proper to provoke further misery by the publication in paperback of *The Satanic Verses*'.

In approaching a number of people who had already declared their views on the general issue, and asking them to summarise their opinions for a newspaper feature on *The Satanic Verses*, *The Independent on Sunday* was behaving quite properly. But in presenting this exercise as though it were a 'poll' it was engaging in a form of journalistic dishonesty which, given the seriousness of the issue, should not be allowed to pass without comment. In reality it would seem that what the paper conducted was not a 'poll' at all but a sham-ballot, whose undeclared purpose was to influence public opinion rather than reflect it, and to do so in a way that fitted in with the paper's editorial view that the paperback should be published, regardless of the consequences.

*

On Tuesday February 6th, two days after the publication of 'In Good Faith' and the feature on the paperback, media coverage reached unprecedented levels as considerable journalistic excitement grew up around the Herbert Read memorial lecture due to be given by Salman Rushdie – and read by his friend Harold Pinter – at the Institute of Contemporary Arts that evening. Salman Rushdie was featured on nearly every major news bulletin that evening, while BBC Radio 4's arts programme *Kaleidoscope* chose the same evening to broadcast an interview with Rushdie which had been recorded a year earlier but which had been frozen after the *fatwa*. The Herbert Read lecture was itself televised in full, and was reported extensively the next morning in practically every daily newspaper. Over the next few days, indeed, it became very difficult to open a daily newspaper without an article, or an editorial or a letter defending Rushdie's right to free speech tumbling into view.

During this week, as had been the case throughout much of the previous year, the defenders of *The Satanic Verses* enjoyed noticeably larger helpings of the freedom of speech they advocated than those Muslims who were supposedly equal beneficiaries. This point was made by Muhammed Aslam Qureshi, the author of one of the five letters which *The Independent on Sunday* published the following week under the heading 'The Muslim case against *The Satanic Verses*'. On the same page the paper published nine somewhat briefer letters defending *The Satanic Verses* and Rushdie's right to free speech. The Muslim response included cogent contributions from Mustaquim Bleher and Professor Syed Ali Ashraf as well as a particularly thoughtful and penetrating letter from Mahmood Jamal:

> The majority of Muslims of the world see fundamentalism as a political rather than a truly religious or spiritual movement and are themselves wary of the intolerance and bigotry of these self-appointed representatives of Muslims.
>
> Salman Rushdie has, from the beginning, got one thing right: that the majority of Muslims are at odds with the minority of authoritarian bigots that plague the Muslim world today. Where he went wrong was that he did not understand the passion with which all Muslims respect and love the Prophet of Islam, regardless of the fact that they be secular, devout or any other kind of Muslim. Indeed, the expression of this extreme devotion is viewed with suspicion by certain fundamentalist quarters!

Had Salman Rushdie written about the above-mentioned bigots or mullahs in a derogatory fashion, he would today enjoy the support of countless numbers of Muslims. His mistake lay in the fact that he chose a rather harsh, one-sided and unbecoming way of dealing with a figure not only revered but much loved by Muslims.

Dissent can be expressed in a variety of ways; by using insults one merely closes the avenue of dialogue just as death threats and violence do. That is why I am not an advocate of the right to insult brands of dissension especially when dealing with the sacred.

By choosing this particular method of expression, for he as a writer did have a choice, he galvanised all Muslim opinion behind the bigots, hence furthering the cause of revivalists and fundamentalist forces within Islam. Is he guilty of naivety, perhaps?

His failure lies in the fact that, whereas in his article and earlier letters he is at pains to explain that he is not against Muslims *per se*, his novel leaves one with the feeling that he meant to insult and injure all Muslims.

One of the great virtues of Jamal's letter was that it looked beyond the novel itself and all merely abstract principles, towards the real political effects which its publication had had within Islam. Something similar could be said of the most forceful contribution to *The Independent on Sunday*'s forum – the open letter to Salman Rushdie from Michael Dummett, the Wykeham Professor of Logic in the University of Oxford, a former Chairman of the Joint Council for the Welfare of Immigrants, who has long been an active campaigner against racial discrimination. Professor Dummett was concerned primarily not with abstract principles which supposedly guarded the freedom of a tiny elite of writers, but with the disastrous effects which the whole affair had had on race relations in this country. His letter was fierce, eloquent and passionate:

Dear Mr Rushdie,

I am extremely glad that the first Muslim responses, published in last Monday's *Independent*, to your article 'In Good Faith' have been so generous. My own reaction, I am sorry to say, is less generous. After a year in which to reflect upon it, is that all you could manage to say?

The 'Rushdie affair' has done untold damage. It has intensified the alienation of Muslims here, and in other Western countries, from the society around them, in reaction to the

uncomprehending liberal chorus of support for you. Racist
hostility towards them, where overt, has been inflamed, and,
where latent, has been aroused.

Professor Dummett went on to acknowledge that a great part of the
blame for this rested with the Ayatollah Khomeini, describing his
fatwa as an abominable act 'supplying to all those prejudiced against
Islam a legitimate ground of accusation'. But he also called upon
Salman Rushdie himself to shoulder his portion of responsibility
and, as a first step along this path, to cease insisting on his right to
have as many readers for his book as possible.

> You have imbibed the assumption of Western intellectuals that
> religious believers may properly be affronted, indeed deserve to
> be affronted. Those in the West who have no religious belief are
> oblivious to the depth of pain caused to those who have by what
> they perceive as blasphemy: lacking so much as the concept of
> something's being holy, they lack the will to grasp the magnitude
> of the affront, although they could begin to imagine it if there is
> anything they hold dear or in respect...

For publishing Professor Dummett's open letter, alongside the
letters from which I have already quoted, and one or two other
commissioned articles which were at least mildly critical of Rushdie,
The Independent on Sunday deserves considerable credit. Yet a
significant part of its good work in starting a real debate about the
Rushdie affair was placed in jeopardy by its own editorial. Although
this was published on the same page as Professor Dummett's open
letter, the arguments advanced in this letter were, like the other
arguments put forward by Muslims in the same paper, loftily
ignored. Instead of seeking to engage in a real debate about the
issue, the writer of the editorial made it clear that his real task was
to carry forward the paper's campaign for a paperback. Although
the editorial began by claiming that it had been the paper's intention
'to marginalise the men who demand Rushdie's death', it now
followed the lead of television and of tabloid newspapers by
pushing the once peripheral figure of Dr Siddiqui into the very
centre of the stage:

> Non-publication of the paperback would do nothing to appease an
> 'Islamic scholar' like Kalim Siddiqui. Anyone who saw Siddiqui on
> television last Friday must surely despair. He wanted the hardback
> withdrawn and Rushdie delivered to an Islamic state where the

author 'would be for the high jump'. Otherwise, he said, British Muslims would 'huff and puff and blow your house down'. He refused to dissociate himself from the *fatwa*, conceding only that it could not be carried out in Britain. Hackles must have risen in millions of living rooms. A man like Siddiqui, coming on like a wolf at the door, serves the cause of racial harmony as badly as the National Front.

Having, however inadvertently, prejudiced its readers against the Muslim cause by giving Dr Siddiqui such unwarranted attention and by its description of him 'coming on like a wolf at the door', *The Independent on Sunday* went on to argue, reasonably enough in some respects, that the law should be invoked in order to prevent any further death-threats against Rushdie:

> Decisive action against such incitements to violence will benefit the Muslim community more than anyone else. It is crucial that they be seen to be not fanatics but people of reason and good will, with genuine grievances against *The Satanic Verses*, as are expressed on these pages, which they are prepared to discuss with its author.

But although Muslim and other dissenting opinion might well be solicited it was only, it would seem, for the paper to ride roughshod over such opinion in pursuit of its own editorial policy. For the editorial went on to advocate immediate publication of a paperback by a 'worldwide conglomerate', bearing on its cover 'a prominent literary health warning' and containing a foreword 'in a tone that is humble as well as fearless, respectful as well as unapologetic'. The only real conciliatory gesture which might have been made – doing without a paperback for the foreseeable future – had clearly been ruled out in advance. Instead the paper commended to its readers a paperback decked out in the tinsel of conciliation.

What was disturbing about this argument was not so much the way in which the newspaper held to its editorial line – which was only to be expected – but that, in the same breath that it called upon Muslims to act as people of reason and engage in serious debate, the newspaper itself declined to join this debate. Indeed, throughout its huge coverage of the issue over the two crucial weeks leading up to the anniversary of the *fatwa*, the complex issue of blasphemy and the law, and the equally complex issue of free speech, were treated by the paper's own editorial staff as though they had been resolved in advance. Dissenting views were solicited and published only to be ignored, and the possibility of any genuine debate developing was stifled almost as soon as it had been canvassed. Although the paper expounded its own position in tones redolent of restraint and moderation, and even expressed the hope that it could create a platform for 'gentleness and reason', its underlying attitude towards the whole issue remained inflexible. Clinging to an absolutist doctrine of free speech with a faith which it declined to submit to rational analysis, it presented a remarkable spectacle which should by now be familiar. For here, once again, we were able to observe the adherents of a quite irrational faith in 'free speech' rebuking Muslims in tones of great intellectual superiority for the supposed fanaticism and irrationality with which they maintained *their* faith. The notion that the Muslim response to the publication of *The Satanic Verses* might conceal an entirely reasonable desire to preserve their human dignity in the face of what they regarded as intolerable insults, was one to which the newspaper appeared unwilling to give serious consideration.

There was, however, an even more significant dimension to the coverage which this edition of the paper gave to Islam. For the same issue of *The Independent on Sunday*, as well as devoting three full pages to coverage of the Rushdie affair, also gave almost an entire page to two separate stories concerning Asian wives under the headline 'Suicide or dowry murder?' These stories concerned dowry customs to be found, according to the first article, 'in some Asian religions'. The article went on to report that the Anti-Dowry campaign had alleged that some suicides among Asian women were actually cases of dowry murder. Although it conceded that there is 'no firm evidence' that husbands or in-laws have committed such murders in Britain, the article did invoke the authority of two academics and gave the impression that they backed its own speculative line of inquiry. Indeed, the article began by claiming that the allegation of dowry murder was 'in part supported by a researcher into the apparently high suicide rate in Britain among women from the Indian subcontinent'. The researcher in question was Dr Veena Soni Raleigh, senior research fellow at the University of Surrey. According to *The Independent on Sunday* a report which she had co-authored showed that women from the Indian sub-continent living in Britain were 'four times more likely to commit suicide than the average woman'. In a somewhat unusual departure from normal journalistic practice, the article went on to quote the views of two junior police officers. In particular it was said that PC Tony Thornton, a coroner's officer in Bradford, 'where there is a large Asian community', was aware of 'two cases where women burned to death in the last two years, but murder was not alleged in either'. He was quoted as saying: 'They were both Pakistani Muslims, and to commit suicide is an insult against their religion. Often we rely on the evidence given by the next of kin, who may have some good reason for doing something they shouldn't.' The implication of these words seems reasonably clear. If committing suicide was an insult to their faith then there was a possibility that these Muslims had actually been murdered. Moreover the words also seemed to imply that, although suicide was against the religion of Muslims, murdering wives or daughters-in-law was not.

This implication was allowed to remain in the article without any editorial comment or correction. While the first article thus identified two women who had burned to death in Bradford in the last two years as 'Pakistani Muslims' and raised as a possibility the idea that they had been murdered by their husbands or relatives, the second article – which clearly had a much stronger factual basis – focused on the case of a woman who alleged that she had been beaten by her husband and bullied into providing a series of dowry 'gifts' from her family to his. She too was identified as a Muslim.

The conjunction of these two articles on a single page in an issue of a newspaper which had devoted three pages to the Rushdie affair should not be passed over in silence. For even if the articles had been based on unimpeachable evidence and accurate journalism, the wisdom of publishing them in such a context is open to question. There is no law against reporting sensitive facts which may easily be misconstrued, nor should there ever be one. For it is right and proper that such matters should be left to the judgment and sensitivity of newspaper editors. But what every good editor recognises, and what all responsible journalists should recognise also, is that it is extremely dangerous to strike the matches of empirical fact too close to the petroleum of prejudice. By the way in which he had apparently allowed a journalist to do just this, the editor of *The Independent on Sunday* had, I believe, committed a grave error of judgment.

In this particular case, however, the error of judgment was even more serious than it might at first appear to be. For the first article in particular was not based on sound evidence and accurate journalism. Dr Raleigh's research, which had been conducted purely into the topic of suicide, did not show that women from the Indian sub-continent were 'four times more likely to commit suicide than the average woman'. This 'fact' rested on a complete misinterpretation of two figures – as a careful reading of the whole report would have made clear. So far as overall suicide levels among women were concerned there was no statistically significant difference between women from the sub-continent and women in general. Suicide levels among women aged 15 to 24 *were* higher in the case of women from the Indian subcontinent, but the level was less than twice that found among women in general.

Because of the way in which her research had been distorted, and the way she had been made to look as though she was endorsing allegations of bride-burning, Dr Raleigh herself immediately contacted the paper to register her alarm and distress.

In the end *The Independent on Sunday* agreed to publish two short paragraphs which gave the correct statistics and in which Dr Raleigh made it clear that none of her research supported allegations of bride-burning and that she would not endorse any such suggestion herself. These paragraphs did not, however, explicitly acknowledge that the paper had misrepresented her statistics. They offered no apology either to Dr Raleigh or to the newspaper's readers.

It was not only Dr Raleigh who was unhappy about the article, however. For PC Thornton also felt that it did not reflect his own words accurately. He told me that he was indeed aware of two cases where women had burned to death in the last two years. But he said that he did not tell the journalist who spoke to him that these women were Muslims and he did not raise the point about suicide being an insult to their faith. He said that both these suggestions had been contributed by the journalist, although he agreed that he may well have accepted them in the belief that she knew better than he did. Indeed, he was happy to admit that he is not an expert on religious affairs and has no knowledge of the attitude of Islam either towards suicide or towards bride burning. PC Thornton said he now felt that he had been wrong even to talk to the journalist from *The Independent on Sunday*. As he somewhat ruefully put it: 'I was caught out'.

In the original article, the quotation from PC Thornton was followed by a quotation from Professor Bhikhu Parekh, Professor of Political Theory at the University of Hull who was at that time Deputy Chairman of the Commission for Racial Equality. This quotation appeared to endorse the speculative line of inquiry followed throughout the article. Yet Professor Parekh was himself extremely concerned by the tone and substance of the article which eventually appeared, and unhappy at the way his words had been taken out of context. He had in fact talked to the journalist concerned for some thirty minutes and he asked her to be particularly cautious in handling the whole subject. In his view the article which the paper published was 'unbalanced and misleading'.

What is perhaps most extraordinary about the two articles is the way in which their conjunction created the impression that dowry is a Muslim custom. For having clearly stated that dowry customs are found 'in some Asian religions' the only religion the articles refer to is Islam. Although neither article explicitly states that dowry murder is a Muslim custom it is this impression which they convey not only to careless readers, but also to quite careful ones.

It is in this regard that the articles are most misleading and most ill-informed. For dowry is not generally associated with Muslims. 'Dowry is not a Muslim custom', says Professor Parekh. It is true that dowry deaths do occur in India, but these happen primarily among Hindus and among Sikhs – and then mainly in a small number of specific communities. Islam itself does not impose dowry. Indeed it inverts the entire dowry system, requiring that the bridegroom's family bestow gifts upon the bride. In Islam, as in every other religious faith, not all believers abide by the strict principles of their religion, and in certain parts of India and in Pakistan it is sometimes the case that Muslims follow local or indigenous marriage customs rather than Islamic ones. What this means in effect is that some Muslims from Pakistan and elsewhere engage in dowry customs in spite of their religion rather than because of it.

The reports which appeared in *The Independent on Sunday*, however, completely ignored these complexities. Instead they implied not only that dowry was a Muslim practice but also that Muslims might, because of their faith, engage in dowry murder. In implying this, and in doing so in a newspaper which had already devoted so much space to its own frequently tendentious coverage of the Rushdie affair, the two articles about dowry customs could only have the effect of fanning the flames of anti-Muslim prejudice. It is quite true that, in comparison to many pieces which have appeared in more popular newspapers, the articles *seemed* restrained. But it is precisely the understated, sober and seemingly factual approach of the first article which makes it so powerful, and so likely to do harm. We should not doubt that the journalist who wrote it had quite other intentions. However naively, she probably believed that her article was furthering the cause of justice and social harmony by exposing acts of cruelty which had previously been concealed. But racialism is frequently spread through idealistic rather than malicious motives and we forget this at our peril.

The two *Independent on Sunday* articles taken together could only give further credence to one of the wildest and most significant misconceptions there is about Islam – namely that dowry murder is in some way a part of the Muslim faith. In this case it would seem that 'Islam' is being treated as a receptacle into which all the ills of Asia – and Africa as well – can be indiscriminately deposited by the ideologists of Western superiority. Much the same process has already taken place over many years in relation to female circumcision and clitoridectomy – a practice which is now frequently treated as though it were essentially an Islamic ritual. It is quite true that clitoridectomy is practised in some Muslim countries – in Egypt and the Sudan for example – and that in these countries the ritual is often incorporated syncretistically into the dominant faith. But it is emphatically not a Koranic ritual or a Muslim custom.

In a climate of opinion where Islam is increasingly treated as an evil force against which all right-thinking liberals should zealously crusade, the tendency to characterise it primarily by rituals and customs which are actually non-Koranic adds up to far more than simple distortion. For the misapprehensions which result have become the fuel out of which the fires of a new form of racial prejudice have been built – prejudice which is based not so much on fantasy as on a kind of distorted empiricism. In this modern form of prejudice a great deal of genuine idealism is mixed up with disguised forms of cultural chauvinism and imperialism. The external and therefore visible patriarchalism of Islam is attacked with a fervour which sometimes seems to be directly proportionate to the degree to which patriarchal and misogynistic attitudes have been internalised *invisibly* in Western culture. In the mirror of Islam we see and persecute the reflection of our own repressiveness, and sometimes do so in the medium of prurient fantasy. Something of the character of this new kind of racialism is conveyed in an anonymous letter which I received recently from a reader of *The Times* in response to a letter of mine which was published there in March 1990:

> All those who have written to *The Times* in praise of ISLAM have been men! To the sniggering amusement of England's indigenous women! Lord Coggan, when Archbishop of Canterbury, once declared 'Islam will enrich our culture': a few pages on in *The Times'* legal columns a report dealt with the action of a Muslim who had challenged the Home Office because he was not permitted to bring his No. 3 wife into the country on No. 2 wife's passport! Enrichment indeed! A few months ago *The Times* reported that a Muslim living in this country with two wives had, with No. 1 wife, been charged with the murder of wife No. 2....
>
> POLYGAMOUS FUCKERY, Kidnap (Waite), Hangings, Bazoft, arranged marriages, petrol dowsing of young brides, circumcision of girl babies, sale of underage girls for a fish-and-chip shop, the acts of barbarism in the name of ISLAM'S 'SIMPLE FAITH' are endless! *Le Monde* commenting on French Muslims' request to marry off their daughters at 12 years of age (sexual deviation) described ISLAM as feudal. Clearly you are looking for trade from the Barbarians and I sincerely hope that your letter encourages a few thousand Muslims and their families to quit southern England and emigrate to Southwold!

What is most disturbing about a letter like this is that the charges which it contains are, in a somewhat more moderate form, in very wide circulation among educated people. In this respect and in others there is a resemblance between modern forms of prejudice against Islam and the ancient charge of ritual murder which, from the Middle Ages onwards, was one of the most important motifs of Christian anti-semitism. Although the charge of ritual murder had no basis in fact, lurid descriptions of this act became central to the complex and spurious 'anthropology' which educated men and women used for centuries to justify the persecution of Jews. Indeed, chief among the early propagators of this anti-semitic legend was no less learned a man than Chaucer, who puts an elaborate story of ritual murder into the mouth of his prioress. To this day there are many venerable and highly respected literary critics who, unable to overcome their reverence for literary tradition, still attempt to teach their students that Chaucer was criticising this legend rather than enthusiastically propagating it.

Such educated disbelief in the capacity of the educated for entertaining cruel and persecutory forms of prejudice is still widespread in our own culture. Because of this there will no doubt be many who simply cannot bring themselves to believe that any quality newspaper in Britain could, even inadvertently and accidentally, publish an article which promoted racial or religious hatred. It is on such civilised disbelief in the very possibility of prejudice and unreason taking root in a culture such as our own that prejudice and unreason thrive and grow strong.

It would nevertheless be quite wrong to write these words while pointing only in the direction of a single newspaper. The coverage given by *The Independent on Sunday* to the Rushdie affair in general and to the issue of dowry deaths in particular certainly did not help to establish an atmosphere of informed and responsible debate. But nearly every other quality newspaper and television channel had, at one time or another during the first year of the *fatwa*, overstepped reasonable criticism of Islam or of Muslims and begun to trespass in the realm of prejudice. As Bhikhu Parekh has written, throughout the early stages of the controversy, most of the national press made little effort to explain the Muslim point of view:

> As so often happens in 'tribal' England, it instinctively ganged up against the Muslims, mocking, abusing, ridiculing and morally bludgeoning then into silence. With several honourable exceptions the racism of many a journalist was just below the surface. They attacked not just the protest, which they were entitled to do, but the entire Muslim community as barbarians unfit to be citizens of a civilised society. The widely used and never clearly defined term 'fundamentalism' became a popularly accepted disguise under which racism masqueraded itself... The term became a devious device for blackmailing Muslims into rejecting their values. Hardly any liberals realised that, in countering Muslim 'fundamentalism', they were setting up a rival fundamentalism of their own and corrupting the great liberal tradition. Historically speaking, whenever liberalism has felt frightened and nervous, it has tended to become aggressive and intolerant. The Rushdie affair was no exception.

As the anniversary of the *fatwa* approached in February 1990, there was still very little coverage in the press which was seriously critical of liberal orthodoxy or more than superficially sympathetic even to the point of view of moderate Muslims. By far the most significant exception to the general trend of press coverage, however, was provided by *The Sunday Correspondent*. On February 11th, the same day that *The Independent on Sunday* carried replies to Salman Rushdie's essay and its article on dowry deaths, *The Sunday Correspondent* published a deeply considered and courageous article by Margaret Hebblethwaite. After condemning the *fatwa*, and arguing that Salman Rushdie was now the victim of a cruel injustice, she went on to look at the other side of the argument: 'A novel which contained inflammatory, anti-semitic language, no matter what its artistic merits, would risk prosecution under the Race Relations Act. Are anti-Islamic and anti-semitic smears so very different?' She went on to point out that the Rushdie affair had created a situation in which Muslims increasingly had to contend with 'sweeping and unjust stereotyping'. Even the quality press proclaimed 'Islam once did intellectual battle. Now it prefers to draw blood.' More than a change of law, Margaret Hebblethwaite wrote, 'we need a change of consciousness, so that such remarks are as socially unacceptable as anti-semitic or anti-black slanders.'

Margaret Hebblethwaite's article provided a welcome relief from the general tone of press coverage of the issue at this time. But that it did not succeed in persuading all her fellow liberals became clear from the issue of *The Guardian* which appeared on February 14th 1990, the anniversary of the *fatwa*. Throughout the previous year the paper had given a great deal of coverage to the Rushdie debate. As one would expect from a great liberal newspaper it had tended to defend the classic doctrines of liberalism and had not always subjected these to as much scrutiny as the circumstances seemed to call for. But, partly because of its carefully nurtured sensitivity to minority communities throughout Britain, dissenting views had frequently been published – not simply, it would seem, out of a strategy of repressive tolerance, but out of a real desire for a genuinely open forum of debate. Tariq Modood's profound and illuminating article 'Alabama Britain', which appeared on 22nd May 1989, was one of several contributions to a debate which was conducted not only in the paper's editorial and correspondence columns, but which also had the appearance of being carried on among the paper's own editorial staff. On February 14th 1990, however, the voice of authoritarian liberalism seemed, for the moment at least, to have won the day. For *The Guardian*'s editorial, 'The year of backing away from the issue', was uncompromising over the question of the paperback. Having asked whether it should be published, the writer of the editorial declined even to consider that various answers might be given to this question:

> The great pending decision is whether there should be a paperback edition of *The Satanic Verses*. There can be only one answer: that paperback must be published. To stop it now would be to give in to terrorism. Obviously, if the author objects, the paperback should be held back. But he wants publication. Ideally – as in Germany and Spain – it should be brought out by a consortium of publishers...

This editorial, together with an article by Keith Vaz which was published in the same issue of the paper, provoked a new round of correspondence in *The Guardian*'s ever open and ever lively correspondence columns. But throughout all this correspondence nobody dared to point out that Germany and Spain were, historically speaking, perhaps not the best examples to follow when it came to questions of how to treat ethnic or religious minorities.

Meanwhile, in the letters column of *The Sunday Correspondent*, it was possible to witness a much more general, and even more serious eclipse of the historical consciousness. For while Margaret Hebblethwaite was congratulated on her article by a young Muslim, a Christian reader from Manchester wrote to object to the 'sophistries and misleading arguments' the article contained. In particular he objected to the parallel between anti-semitic and anti-Islamic smears, arguing that while anti-semitic statements are wrong because they are based on race, anti-Islamic statements should be tolerated because they express only an 'aversion to a particular religion'.

This letter would be horrifying were it not for the fact that the historical innocence it expresses is so widespread. In the face of such uninformed attitudes, perhaps it really is time for modern historians of anti-semitism to shout from the rooftops the conclusion which they have buried in academic treatises: namely that modern racial anti-semitism is, in its historical origins, a fundamentally religious phenomenon which has its roots in the profound hatred of Judaism which was cultivated by the Christian church over a period of very many centuries.

As the anniversary of the *fatwa*, so long heralded in the media, finally came, this point, which should have been at the forefront of the debate, was not made at all.

CHAPTER FIVE

On Not Burning Your Enemy's Flag

In the last two chapters I have managed to discuss only a fraction of the coverage the *Satanic Verses* affair received during the weeks which led up to the first anniversary of the *fatwa*. For during this period the whole issue received attention not only in newspapers, magazines and periodicals, but also on radio and television. Throughout this coverage, as is the way with anniversaries, a great many people spent a great deal of time remembering history. But, as the column inches and broadcasting hours multiplied, it became increasingly clear that we were forgetting a good deal of history as well. For very few commentators took the trouble to recall that the *Satanic Verses* affair did not begin on February 14th 1989, or even a month earlier when a copy of the book was burnt in Bradford. The Muslim campaign against *The Satanic Verses* started almost as soon as the book was published in September 1988. And what is even more significant is that it was initially an entirely peaceful campaign, conducted in the best traditions of British democracy by letters, by lobbying, by pleading, and even by a high-level diplomatic initiative.

It was only when all means of peaceful democratic protest had been exhausted, when Muslim leaders had knocked on the doors of the High Court and found that they were barred against them, when their impassioned letters had been ignored by the author, and treated by the publishers with high literary disdain, that groups of Muslims in Bolton and in Bradford made their fateful decision to burn a copy of Salman Rushdie's book in order to draw attention to their campaign.

The book-burning was, of course, immediately compared to Nazi outrages. But, as many have pointed out since, the comparison is unjust. For it was the act not of a contemptuous and powerful political organisation, but of a minority who had long been victims of racialism themselves and who were expressing, as much as anything else, rage at their own sense of frustration and powerlessness.

We should not doubt that, by intention at least, the Muslims who burnt a copy of *The Satanic Verses* were also seeking to express love – a fierce and uncompromising love for Islam and for the Prophet Muhammad who they felt had been insulted and reviled. But as soon as the icon of the burning book became separated from this intention, the gesture could only be construed as one expressing contempt, hatred, and a callous insensitivity to Western feelings. That is why something which was intended as an affirmation of the sacred aroused such outrage. This outrage was, as I think the vast majority of moderate British Muslims have now recognised, entirely authentic and, in a society where books and the written word tend themselves to be regarded as sacred, entirely understandable. While a number of responsible Muslims, both in Bradford and elsewhere, defend the bookburning on the grounds that such an extreme gesture was necessary at the time, it is notable that the gesture has not been repeated.

What is most disturbing about the *Satanic Verses* affair, however, is that the sensitivity of Muslims to our most sacred beliefs, however reluctantly it has been acquired, has not been matched by our sensitivity to theirs.

In his essay 'In Good Faith', Rushdie tried, as we have seen, to justify the offence he has given by explaining his intentions. There seems to be no doubt at all that he did intend, with that rather cold and rational idealism to which post-modernist and post-Marxist artists have increasingly succumbed, that his book should be read as a hymn of love, a celebration both of the sacredness of art and of a utopian vision of society, in which the boundaries of race, class, sex and nationality melt mysteriously away. Nor would it be reasonable to claim that Rushdie's account of his own intentions is irrelevant to our understanding of the novel. But his account of what he thought he was doing is, in the end, no *more* relevant to his work of art than are the holy intentions of the Bradford Council of Mosques to the act of book-burning which they sanctioned. For novels do not go out into the world tied to the nursemaid of their authors' intentions. Indeed the novel has perhaps always been a much harder, more self-sufficient and more dangerous art form than we like to think. If a novel seems to contain, woven into its rich imaginative complexity, contempt, hatred and scorn, and if the novel's readers respond to these emotions with greater imaginative sensitivity than the author himself, the author might well be right to ask whether his readers are not being over-sensitive. But he might also do well to ask whether he has not himself been insensitive, and to remember that there is a long history of messiahs who preach gospels of utopian harmony but who succeed only in producing disharmony.

There is certainly no good reason to suppose that Rushdie's decision to address his audience at such length from the powerful platforms provided by *The Independent on Sunday* and the Institute of Contemporary Arts, has done anything to defuse this tragic conflict. Instead, such lofty literary platforms have helped to preserve the air of unreality which has surrounded the whole debate from its inception.

For, as we have seen, participants in this debate have again and again talked as though the tradition of free speech is an abstract principle, formulated primarily for the benefit of a small elite of intellectuals and artists. This modern manifestation of the ancient religious principle of *contemptus mundi* is illustrated clearly by the attitude towards freedom of expression which is implicit in the pamphlet on blasphemy produced by the International Committee for the Defence of Salman Rushdie – the same pamphlet which provided one of the starting points for this book.

Although it is quite clearly concerned with the general issue of legal restraints on freedom of expression, the entire document is written as though its authors inhabit a world where no such restraints exist other than the laws of blasphemy which they are proposing to abolish. The real political and historical world in which libel laws, race relations laws and obscenity laws have long existed is, as it were, annihilated by the almost religious passion with which the authors pursue their apocalyptic vision of another world than this, where freedom of expression is absolute and untrammelled by any restrictions whatsoever.

There can be no doubt that such zeal for free expression can be used to bring real political benefits, particularly when it is harnessed to campaigns against the censorship imposed by tyrannical or autocratic governments. In this respect it is quite clear that free speech pressure groups, such as Article 19, have done much good work, both in relation to foreign governments and to our own.

But one of the great failures of Article 19, and of other valuable organisations such as the Rationalist Press Association, is their reluctance to discriminate between the freedom to impart information and the freedom to insult, offend or abuse. In the rational utopia they look forward to it would seem that everybody would be free to abuse and insult everybody else and nobody would take offence. Words would not wound, insults would not hurt, and abuse, however obscene, would provoke neither anger nor violence.

But in the real political world which we all perforce inhabit, words *do* wound, insults *do* hurt, and abuse – especially extreme and obscene abuse – *does* provoke both anger and violence. Until recently our own tradition of free speech has nearly always recognised this, which is why the unwritten constitution of our freedom has shied away from absolutist doctrines of liberty and assumed instead that with freedom there comes responsibility. In the words of Anthony Lejeune, 'Writers, speakers, indeed all of us, have responsibilities – moral, prudential, conventional or simply a matter of good taste – covering areas much wider than the law can or should constrain'. It is because these responsibilities are so complex, and because absolutist doctrines of free speech are so dangerous, that the crusade for unconditional free expression, launched in response to Muslim protests against *The Satanic Verses*, needs to be halted for a while at least.

It is because we so badly need to pause for thought, and to pause for a very considerable time, that the question of whether *The Satanic Verses* should appear in paperback merits even more debate than it has already had.

It would certainly seem reasonable to suggest that *The Satanic Verses*, which is by common consent an extraordinary book, should not be treated as though it were an ordinary one. There are in particular three pressing arguments why it should *not* be brought out as a paperback in the foreseeable future.

In the first place it should be recognised that, although as a society we do tolerate the publication of many offensive books, the most common victims of prejudice, including women, blacks, Jews and homosexuals, tend to be protected by a strong liberal consensus, and have the support of many influential individuals in the media and elsewhere. Muslims, for the most part, enjoy no such protection.

In the second place we should recognise that there is a huge moral difference between, as it were, accidentally publishing a book in hardback which gives offence on an unprecedented scale, and quite deliberately issuing the book later in paperback in the full knowledge of the added offence this would cause. To Muslims defending their faith in Muhammad it would be rather like the difference between manslaughter and murder.

In the third place, as Shabbir Akhtar wrote recently in *The Independent on Sunday*, the present situation has the advantage of allowing both sides to feel that they have achieved a limited victory. We have reached, in other words, something very close to the kind of stalemate in which a fruitful dialogue can begin. If the paperback is now published this dialogue will be interrupted by a new uproar in which calm and reasonable voices will not be heard.

There are, of course, a number of counter-arguments to the view that *The Satanic Verses* should not be published in paperback. Many people believe that it would be wrong to make the kind of concession to Muslim sensitivities that we do not generally make to Christian ones. One of the factors which this view ignores is that Muslim and Christian sensitivities are different. Christians, it must be observed, sometimes seem to take a perverse pleasure in exposing their own faith to the greatest possible abuse, and suffering this abuse without flinching. To turn the other cheek in the face of abuse or blasphemy is, after all, to engage in *imitatio Christi*. Islam does not have the same tradition of suffering insults passively, and there would seem to be no good grounds why Christians – or post-Christian rationalists – should seek to impose on Muslims their own theologically grounded passivity.

But, even if we ignore the difference between Muslim and Christian attitudes, the case for disregarding Muslim objections to the paperback still does not hold. The precedent set by Allen Lane over Siné's *Massacre* has already been cited. But there are other precedents too. Much more recently, in the latter part of 1987, the trade press reported that the most highly regarded bookseller in Britain, Tim Waterstone, had decided as a matter of policy that his shops would not stock Jeremy Pascall's book *God: The Ultimate Autobiography* on the grounds that Christians might find it offensive. In February 1990, however, Tim Waterstone argued in the pages of *The Independent on Sunday* that *The Satanic Verses* should be published in paperback in spite of the offence it has caused to Muslims. It is little wonder that Shabbir Akhtar has complained of what he calls 'the double or even triple moral standards' which tend to be operated by the defenders of free speech.

The same kind of moral slippage is evident in another argument which was frequently advanced by those who, in the early part of 1990, pressed for the immediate publication of *The Satanic Verses* in paperback. For again and again we were told that to refrain from putting *The Satanic Verses* into paperback would be to play into the hands of fundamentalists by capitulating to terrorist threats. Have those who put forward this view paused for a moment to ponder on its implications? What would happen if the same facile moral logic were applied to the problem of apartheid in South Africa? Should we refuse to recognise the black community's rage for justice simply because that rage has sometimes found expression in terrorist acts? Would it not be better to recognise that the dilemma which is posed by terrorism is not a religious or apocalyptic one, in which all governments and other victims of terrorism are God-like and good, and all terrorists are evil and of the devil? It is a moral dilemma, which can only be solved by weighing very carefully the moral and political issues which are involved in each particular case.

The *fatwa* pronounced by the Ayatollah Khomeini was indeed cruel, tyrannical and murderous, and as a result Salman Rushdie is now the victim of a great injustice. But widespread Muslim protests against the book started long before the Ayatollah showed any concern about it, and the grounds of these protests have not changed since. Before the *fatwa*, the protests were ignored, if we are honest about the matter, for the simple reason that the opinions and feelings of Muslims do not count for very much in this country, and indeed are held in contempt by many. After the *fatwa* the views and feelings of British Muslims continued to be ignored by most people for exactly the same reasons. Except that now the *fatwa* could be cited as a pretext for refusing to consider the Muslim case. The Ayatollah's cruel pronouncement, over which ordinary Muslims had no control, thus came to be used as an excuse for ignoring the feelings of British Muslims, in just the same way that abhorrence for IRA violence has been used for many years as a pretext for ignoring the aspirations and grievances of ordinary Irish Catholics. When some British Muslims, feeling deeply threatened by the liberal backlash against them, began to shelter behind the *fatwa* and to endorse it in public themselves, hard-line liberals were merely given further grounds for continuing to treat their views with contempt.

The argument that the paperback must be published in order to show that we will not capitulate to terrorism may seem reasonable. But if we inspect it more carefully it begins to seem that those who advance it may themselves have capitulated. For, faced with the threat of real violence, a number of intellectuals have indeed reacted with terror. They have fallen into a kind of moral panic in which serious thought and all moral and intellectual analysis have become impossible. In this atmosphere of moral terror, they can respond to threats only by counterthreats or by the triumphalist proposal to publish the book immediately in paperback. Paralysed by their own fear, they cannot understand that such a move would only deepen the cycle of violence.

Of course there are occasions when terrorism should be resisted without compromise. But if we have not learnt by now that the most common cause of terrorism is the denial of natural justice, and that those who insist on perpetuating such a denial are the ones who are perpetuating terrorism, then we have not learnt one of the most important lessons which history has to teach.

The reason why this lesson should now be learnt quickly is provided, I believe, by the depth and strength of the racialism which exists in our society. In Bradford, as we have seen, the Rushdie affair has already caused enormous damage to race relations, and racialist feelings, which were always latent, were expressed with some violence during 1989. Such developments have by no means been restricted to Bradford but have taken place in almost all areas with a high Muslim population. In London, to cite one small but significant example, the words 'KILL A MUSLIM FOR CHRISTMAS' appeared during the latter part of 1989 daubed over the walls of a tube station. Elsewhere 'GAS THE MUSLIMS' has appeared as graffiti.

That Salman Rushdie is himself aware of at least some of these developments was made clear in the interview he gave to *The Independent on Sunday* in February 1990, where he was quoted as saying 'Any abuse directed against Muslims makes me as angry as it makes them'. Yet his only real reference to the huge damage caused to race relations in Britain by the *Satanic Verses* affair was a brief paragraph in his interview, in which he discussed the intentions which lay behind his essay 'In Good Faith': 'I wanted to explain that with the events of the last year my responses have in many cases been very similar to those of the Muslim people attacking me: I'm horrified that the National Front could use my name as a way of taunting Asians and I wanted to make it clear: that's not my team, they're not my supporters.'

The thought that Salman Rushdie seemed quite unable to entertain was that he might actually have contributed to provoking racial violence. When in his essay he writes that 'I have never given the least comfort or encouragement to racists', it would seem that he has genuinely failed to understand the complexities and the consequences of his own actions. For while it is undoubtedly true that Rushdie has never consciously given *encouragement* to racists, it would seem to be undeniably true that his book, and his uncompromising stance throughout the ensuing debate, *has* given a great deal of unintended *comfort* to racists. The fact that Rushdie has always been an ideological opponent of racism does not alter the case at all. There are enough examples of extreme ideological anti-racism which have turned into forms of unintended racism to caution us against reposing too much faith in professions of ideological allegiance.

This is not to say that Rushdie himself should be held primarily responsible for any violence which has taken place in the wake of the *Satanic Verses* affair. For the chain of causality is a complex one and we should be scrupulously careful to avoid making Salman Rushdie the scapegoat for what is, when all is said and done, the racialism of *our* society. But given the fact that racialism in Britain is a lot stronger than we sometimes care to admit, it does seem reasonable to expect novelists, especially novelists who deal with racially sensitive subjects, to be prepared on occasion to lay aside the role of the artist – which is sometimes a little cold and even a little cruel – and show instead ordinary human sensitivity.

Even in this regard, however, it would be quite wrong to ask Salman Rushdie to bear the whole responsibility for failing to show such sensitivity. For the act of writing and publishing a novel, however lonely it may sometimes seem to the artist concerned, is not a purely individual act. It is a cultural act in which individual artists, though they may vaunt their 'originality' or be celebrated for it, are deeply conditioned by the literary and cultural traditions which they inherit and by the environment of critical assumptions in which they cannot but work. In view of the cold rigidity of much recent literary theory, and the almost systematic insensitivity of post-modernist and post-structuralist criticism, to ask that an artist should exhibit 'ordinary human sensitivity' is to ask a very great deal.

Indeed, so bizarre and obsolete will this term seem to many post-modern literary intellectuals that it is, perhaps, necessary to offer some assistance with it. In this respect we could do worse than enlist the help of a letter from Anthony Lejeune which was published in February 1990 by *The Daily Telegraph*. The letter was a response to a claim which had been made in the paper by Anthony Burgess, who wrote: 'Writers like myself are too timid to outrage with blasphemy, and discretion has sometimes damaged our art.' Lejeune was sceptical about this claim:

> Is timidity really the sole reason for his not outraging other people's feelings? Does art automatically justify any cause of outrage? There are certain beliefs, and certain symbols of such beliefs (an enemy's flag perhaps), which I personally would wish to treat with respect simply because human beings have loved them and died for them.

Lejeune's words express what is perhaps the crux of the entire *Satanic Verses* affair. For, by insulting the sacred tradition of the Koran and by burning books, what both parties in this dispute have shown is a callous disregard for each other's most sacred symbols and most precious feelings. Instead of respecting these feelings, both camps have burnt each other's flags, with the result that a vicious circle of offence, outrage and anger has developed. So long as the conflict remains unresolved this vicious circle of hatred will continue, and we should not underestimate how serious and tragic its long term effects might be.

It was the Jewish poet Heinrich Heine who said that people who start by burning books will end by burning people, and his words have already received a measure of confirmation in the way that the Muslim campaign against Salman Rushdie has progressed.

The rigidity of some forms of Islamic fundamentalism is real, as is their potential for cruelty. But we should also recognise that absolutist doctrines of freedom are themselves rigid, and that, in the four decades which have passed since the Second World War, we have developed an intellectual culture which has many marks of insensitivity and callousness, and which itself has an enormous potential for cruelty. Perhaps it is time to develop Heinrich Heine's insight and recognise that if, as a society, we give encouragement to those who claim a high and holy right to injure the most precious religious feelings of Muslims, then some people will inevitably interpret this as a licence to injure Muslims. For confirmation that this has begun to happen already we need only refer back to the words of Mamoor Khan in Julie Flint's *Observer* article.

Racialism is always at its most vicious in those cultural situations where a tacit or unconscious alliance develops between intellectuals and the perpetrators of street-violence. One of the most disturbing features of the *Satanic Verses* affair is that just such an alliance seems already to have emerged.

I do not blame Salman Rushdie for not recognising this. The fault is not his but ours for creating a culture which is insensitive to the power of insult and in which, as Michael Dummett pointed out in his open letter, intellectuals have sanctified the assumption 'that religious believers may properly be affronted, indeed deserve to be affronted'. As an atheist who was brought up as a Methodist I share neither Professor Dummett's Roman Catholic perspective nor his Christian faith. But I do share his concern at the callousness and insensitivity of the intellectual culture we have created. It is time we recognised that when we plunge the dagger of our own intellectual superiority into other people's religious faith, we are engaging in a form of intellectual cruelty which is also a form of real cruelty.

If we insult religious believers in this way, we are not demonstrating intellectual independence or proving that we have emancipated ourselves from our religious heritage. For, as I have already argued, one of the most distinctive characteristics of Judaeo-Christian monotheism is the contempt in which it holds other people's religious faith. If we secularise such religious intolerance and present it as a form of rationalist humanism we are in effect perpetuating one of the worst features of our religious tradition. If, marching under the banner of crusading humanism, we not only insult religious believers, but compound the insult with obscenity, we are doing something which is profoundly repressive and profoundly destructive. For most religions do not disintegrate when they are insulted. They almost invariably internalise the hurt which is inflicted on them and grow more rigid and more cruel.

If we really want to make Islam into the most cruel and tyrannical religion there has ever been, we should go on insulting it as the West has been doing for very many centuries, and as Salman Rushdie is now doing on our behalf. If, however, we are at all interested in the future and vitality of our own culture, in respecting the dignity of Muslims, and in preserving ordinary human sensitivity, we should decide that we can do without a paperback of *The Satanic Verses*. We should also start to face up to our own responsibilities and recognise that Salman Rushdie has been betrayed into his terrible ordeal not primarily by *his* insensitivity but by *ours*.

To ask, as I have asked throughout this book, that we should recognise the internalised cruelty of our own intellectual culture is to ask a great deal. In this century alone it might seem that we have had quite enough difficulty recognising the cruelty of other cultures and other regimes without being called on to recognise the cruelty of our own. In 1944, the former Soviet official Victor Kravchenko sought in his political autobiography to convey the extent of the tragedy which had been brought about by Stalin in Russia. Having given statistics for the millions who were arrested, exiled or executed in the Great Purge, he wrote:

> But even these colossal figures don't sum up the tragedy. They're big but they are cold. Their very immensity makes them a bit unreal. One must think of the victims not in such impersonal terms, but as individuals. One must recall that each of these multitudes had relatives, friends, dependants who shared his sufferings; that each of them had hopes, plans, actual achievements which were shattered. To the historian of tomorrow, to the sociologist of today, these are statistics. But to me, who lived through it, the digits have bodies and minds and souls, all of which were hurt, outraged and humiliated.

Kravchenko's words convey in vivid and urgent terms something of the hugeness of the human tragedy which was still being played out inside Stalin's Soviet Union as he wrote. But when his autobiography *I Chose Freedom* was published in the West in 1947, it was widely believed to be a political forgery designed by agents of the capitalist West to discredit Marxism and communism. Many western intellectuals simply could not bring themselves to believe that any communist leader could be capable of such cruelty.

Some years earlier George Orwell had emerged as one of the few writers on the left who *was* able to believe such things. The socialist historian R.H. Tawney, who, like the historian E.P. Thompson, kept his faith in Stalin much longer, once asked, 'How does Orwell *know* that things in the Soviet Union are so bad?' The answer to Tawney's question is that Orwell used his imagination. Above all, having used his imagination to understand the strength of his own violent impulses, and the depth of his own cruelty, he was able to believe in the reality of other people's violence, and in their capacity to torture and to kill for the sake of an ideal. Other intellectuals on the left, because they could not imagine violence and feel the reality of their own cruelty, could not recognise violence in others. It was partly for this reason that they could not believe in the reality of the tyranny which Stalin had instituted.

The same pattern of educated disbelief in other people's violence can be discerned in relation to Hitler's regime in Germany. The very scale of the destruction wrought by Hitler almost inevitably aroused unconscious denial. In the early years of the Second World War, Richard Lichtheim, a member of the Jewish community in Geneva, could see clearly what was happening to his fellow Jews in Germany. He could see but he could not persuade others of the truth of what he saw. In 1942 he replied to a Jewish organisation in America who had asked him to 'review the position of the Jews in Europe':

> You wanted facts and figures. Have I stated the facts? Some of them, but very few. Think of the facts behind the facts, of the rivers of tears and streams of blood, the broken limbs and the naked bodies, the bleeding feet and the crying children, the stench and the filth, the biting cold and the gnawing hunger, the black despair in millions of hearts...I have written 4,000 words and I have said nothing. Use your imagination, friend.

To compare the plight of Muslims in Britain in the 1990s with the predicament of European Jews earlier this century, or of Stalin's victims, may seem to some inappropriate. For these were tragedies on a scale so huge that before they happened they were quite unimaginable.

But it was precisely because they were unimaginable that these tragedies did take place, and it is because the reluctance to imagine violence is still one of the most notable characteristics of our own political and literary intelligentsia that we need to resist the temptation to treat the Rushdie affair merely as an unfortunate episode of literary history.

It is certainly true that, when placed alongside the castastrophes brought about in Europe earlier this century by Stalin and Hitler, the Rushdie affair in itself would seem to be little more than a local skirmish. For although it has had international repercussions its most serious effects have been in Britain and in certain Muslim communities in the Indian subcontinent. Ultimately, however, what started as a dispute about literature cannot be separated from the much larger crisis in the relationship between Islam and the West.

The latest phase of what is, historically, a continuing crisis may be traced back at least to the foundation of the state of Israel in 1945. But the crisis has deepened immeasurably during the past twenty years, partly as a result of political developments in Iran. Britain and America have themselves played a very large role in shaping these developments. For it was by disregarding Iranian nationalist aspirations and sustaining instead Westward-looking regimes that first Britain and then the United States constructed the gallows from which a whole generation of hostages and innocent religious and political dissidents would subsequently be strung.

Britain's most decisive intervention in the internal politics of Iran was made in 1921, when it backed Colonel Reza Khan, the founder of the Pahlavi dynasty, in his successful attempt to wrest power from the older Qajar dynasty. One of Britain's main motives was to continue its exploitation of Iranian oil in order to fuel the Royal Navy. To this end it first actively supported, and then tolerated, an anti-Islamic regime led by a Westernising tyrant who sought to destroy the Semitic heritage of Iran and take it back to its 'Aryan' roots.

Britain's relationship with Iran began to break down as Shah Reza moved closer and closer to Hitler. The Shah was forced into exile in 1941. He was replaced, however, by his son Muhammad Reza under whom Iran became a client state of the United States. The regime of the new Shah developed into a cruel tyranny. It was sustained internally by torture and the systematic execution or incarceration of the Shah's opponents. It was sustained externally by the CIA and by American political, economic and diplomatic support.

It was primarily because of the legacy of hatred left in Iran by Britain, America and other imperialist powers that Khomeini was able to mobilise massive popular support for a revolution which would end in tyranny and repression on an even greater scale than had been seen under the Shahs. One factor which was crucial to the mass-psychology of this revolution was Khomeini's demonisation of America, which was consistently portrayed as 'the Great Satan'. But, instead of taking responsibility for the consequences of their own actions, Britain, and above all America, responded in kind by effectively demonising the Ayatollah Khomeini. They sometimes demonised not only Khomeini but all those Shiite Muslims who followed him, and even the vast majority of Sunni Muslims who owe him no allegiance. In moments of extremity which soon became accepted as normal we began to demonise Islam itself. Increasingly, as had been the case centuries earlier, Islam was portrayed not as the heterogeneous faith it is, but as a murderous and tyrannical religion, the quintessence of all cruelty.

This process of demonisation belonged essentially to the realm of fantasy, as can be seen clearly enough from an example of anti-Muslim rhetoric which appeared in *The Star* in February 1989 and which is quoted by Malise Ruthven in his *A Satanic Affair*:

> Isn't the world getting sick of the ranting that pours non-stop from the disgusting foam-flecked lips of the Ayatollah Khomeini? Clearly this Muslim cleric is stark raving mad. And more dangerous than a rabid dog. Surely the tragedy is that millions of his misguided and equally potty followers believe every word of hatred he hisses through those yellow stained teeth. The terrifying thing is not that a lot of these crackpots actually live here among us in Britain, but that we are actually becoming frightened of them. The whole thing is crazy. And it has to stop.

But, like all examples of modern political demonology, this kind of negative stereotyping has been significantly strengthened by a kind of distorted empiricism. In particular, the perception of Islam as a cruel and murderous religion has been reinforced by a number of political developments both in Pakistan and in the Middle East.

In Pakistan the extreme right-wing Jamaat-i-Islami movement had emerged during the 1950s under the leadership of Maulana Abu'l Ala Maududi. Although Maududi presented himself as an Islamic 'fundamentalist', his own political philosophy had been strongly influenced by Western thinkers including Hitler and Mussolini. During the early 1970s both he and his followers were strong supporters of General Zia's Islamisation policies, strengthening the Western perception of Islam as an essentially repressive religion. Meanwhile, in the Middle East, the emergence of Palestinian terrorism during the late 1960s, and the adoption by some Palestinian activists of Western anti-semitic propaganda, were further factors in persuading some Western observers to regard Islam as a cruel and essentially evil religion. The fact that the new forms of Arab anti-semitism had been manufactured in Christian Europe over a period of centuries, and had only recently been exported to the Middle East, was disregarded. Some commentators even began to talk as though anti-semitism was one of the traditions of Islam. More recently the Iran-Iraq war, the sudden discovery by the media after Farzad Bazoft's death of the long-standing tyranny in Iraq, and the emergence of 'Islamic' tyrannies in countries like the Sudan have all helped to add more fuel to Western anti-Islamic prejudice.

Again and again Western observers have sought to 'construct' the character of Islam by focusing on the most extreme and repressive practices of Islamic states or organisations and disregarding all other factors. If we were to adopt the same attitude towards Western history, then it would undoubtedly be necessary to regard Stalin, who was educated in a seminary, as the creator of a Christian regime, and Hitler, who was brought up as a Roman Catholic, as a Christian statesman. The fact that both Stalin and Hitler persecuted those Christians who opposed their regimes merely serves to strengthen the analogy. For in recent years 'Islamic' tyrants such as Khomeini in Iran and General Zia in Pakistan have themselves persecuted the many faithful Muslims who have opposed them. Western observers are reluctant to acknowledge such facts and in general seem quite unwilling to recognise that Islam, like any other ancient faith, is profoundly heterogeneous. Instead, they have sought again and again to force upon a faith which has often shown great religious tolerance, a narrow stereotype which portrays it and all its works as the quintessence of cruelty and intolerance.

The injustice and the inconsistency which underlie Western reactions to political developments in Islam have been unveiled with considerable shrewdness by the leader of the Ahmadis, now regarded within Islam as a non-Muslim sect. In his book *Murder in the Name of Allah*, Mirza Tahir Ahmad concludes a discussion of this question with the following words:

> In Lebanon, there have been Muslim terrorists and Christian terrorists, and also Israeli agents and soldiers involved at one time or another in terrorist activities which appal human sensibilities. But you will not hear of Jewish or Christian terrorism in relation to what is happening in Lebanon. All acts of violence are put together and wrapped up in the package of 'Islamic terrorism'.
>
> The conduct of adherents of every religion varies from country to country, from sect to sect, from age to age, and from person to person. How very different is the conduct of Jesus's disciples from those in Pinochet's Chile, or in South Africa, who claim to uphold Christian values. Which is to represent Christianity? Are we entitled to describe the First and Second World Wars, in which millions of people lost their lives, as Christian wars against humanity?
>
> …Any act of war in a Muslim country is perceived in the West as the extension of 'Islamic terrorism' but in any other country such an act is seen as a political dispute. Why must such dual standards of justice prevail? One really begins to wonder if there is an undercurrent of hatred for Islam beneath the apparently calm surface of Christian civilisation. Is it perhaps a hangover from centuries of Crusades against Muslim powers, or is it the old wine of the orientalists' venom against Islam served in new goblets?

Salman Rushdie's *The Satanic Verses* is perceived in the Muslim world as the latest goblet in which the old wine of the orientalists' venom has been served up. It is because it belongs to a much larger 'undercurrent of hatred for Islam' that it remains, for all the conciliatory words which have recently been spoken by its author, such a disturbing book.

Without the undercurrent of hatred, and the general crisis in the relationship between the West and Islam which pre-existed the book, there would scarcely be any cause for concern. But, largely because of the context of hatred in which it was written and published, it has had the effect of deepening the crisis. It has done so with such dramatic effect that it does not now seem completely inappropriate to compare the plight of Muslims today with the predicament of the Jews of Europe. For if the West continues to refine and develop the forms of demonological anti-Islamic prejudice which have emerged since 1945, and if it continues on a course of confrontation with Islam in general, or with Iran in particular, then the kind of conflict which might ultimately arise would be on a huge scale. It is precisely because many would wish to characterise such a huge conflict as 'unimaginable' that we should endeavour to imagine it.

It must of course be conceded that although there are many similarities between the plight of Muslims today and the predicament of European Jews some sixty years ago, there are also many important differences. Above all it would be difficult for anyone to charge British Muslims with having developed the kind of ghetto mentality which, in the deeply considered view of Bruno Bettelheim, himself a Jew who suffered under Hitler, made them share some of the blame for the Holocaust itself:

> It was inertia that led millions of Jews into the ghettos the SS created for them. It was inertia that made hundreds of thousands sit home waiting for their executioners... It was part of ghetto thinking when, after the boycott of Jewish places of business, individual Jews and organisations proclaimed, contrary to the truth, that they had not been molested. It was ghetto thinking when German Jews objected to the truth about their mistreatment being made public and when Jewish organisations in Germany objected to the answering American Jewish boycott of German goods. They were motivated by anxiety and a desire to curry favour.
>
> That is exactly what ghetto thinking is: to believe that one can ingratiate oneself with a mortal enemy by denying that his lashes sting, to deny one's own degradation in return for a moment's respite, to support one's enemy who will only use his strength the better to destroy one. All this is part of the ghetto philosophy.

British Muslims, like many Muslims elsewhere in Europe, particulary in France and Germany where anti-Muslim prejudice is extremely well developed, have not for the most part fallen victim to this kind of ghetto thinking. They have felt the lashes of Western contempt for Islam keenly, but they have not tried to pretend that these lashes do not sting. Rather they have expressed both their pain and their anger through acts such as the book- burning in Bradford. We may resent such attacks on our sacred beliefs, but in the end we should perhaps be grateful for them. For without the determined Muslim campaign against *The Satanic Verses* it would be quite impossible for an intellectual culture as insensitive as our own even to begin to understand the depth of the hurt it is capable, through words alone, of inflicting upon another culture.

At the same time, however, we should recognise that the Muslim response to the book, necessary though it was, has succeeded, to some extent at least, in doing precisely what Jewish quietists feared they might do in the 1930s if they reacted angrily to anti-semitic insults. For by responding in the way they have, British Muslims have actually succeeded in intensifying the prejudice against them which already existed.

The noose of anti-Islamic prejudice was tied long ago. But the events which took place in Britain during 1989 have succeeded in putting the heads of hundreds of thousands of British Muslims inside that noose. That is why we must now begin to untie it. We should not underestimate how difficult this task will be, nor how long it will take. At the same time, however, we should be wary of replacing the West's irrational intolerance of Islam and all its works with an equally irrational and indiscriminate love of Islam. The consequences of inverting prejudice in this way can be seen all too clearly in the history of European and American attitudes towards Jews in this century. For what has happened in many quarters is that a profound and irrational anti-semitism has been replaced by an attitude which amounts to philo-semitism; in both Britain and America there has sometimes been a reluctance to criticise any Jewish or Israeli act and a tendency to release both Israeli politicians and Israeli soldiers from the normal constraints of political morality.

When anti-semitism is inverted in this way it should be noted that the main victims of the new upside-down prejudice are, once again, Jews. For to the extent that Britain, America and other Western powers have refrained from opposing the aggressive expansionism of right-wing politicians in Israel, to that extent have they helped to betray moderate Israelis, who genuinely seek accommodation with Palestinians, into the hands of hard-line politicians who are intent only on the ruthless subjugation of Arab 'terrorists'. This in turn has strengthened the perception of Jews as intolerant and supremacist and has itself contributed to the current resurgence of anti-semitism in Europe.

Any tendency to invert anti-Islamic prejudice in the same way would be likely to have similar results. For we should not shy away from the fact that there are, both in this country and throughout the world, a significant number of Muslims who do preach an extreme, intolerant and supremacist version of their faith. Until the Rushdie affair the influence of such extremists in this country was minute. But the publication of *The Satanic Verses* and, to use Michael Dummett's phrase, 'the uncomprehending chorus of liberal support for it' have had the effect of driving many moderate Muslims into the strong and seemingly secure arms of these extremists. If a significant number of British liberals and members of the literary intelligentsia now re-align themselves, this will in itself repair some of the damage which has been done to the cause of moderation. But it is extremely important that we should not, in an attempt to undo the harm which has already been caused, surrender the moral right to criticise the small number of Muslim extremists in this country and the much larger number abroad who are sometimes as skilled in the dissemination of hatred as extremist Christians, extremist Jews or indeed, extremist secularists. For to invert anti-Islamic prejudice in this way could, in the long term, do almost as much harm to the cause of Muslim moderation as direct forms of prejudice are doing at the moment.

These direct forms of prejudice have already caused great damage to community relations in many British towns and cities. As we have seen, real violence has already broken out in the streets of Bradford and elsewhere, and the violence of young white teenagers has been met with a violent response from those they have attacked. Partly because Penguin has so far refrained from publishing the paperback and partly because of the efforts of local church and community workers who are *not* blinded by prejudice, this violence has not got out of control. But the danger which remains is that it may, and that if it did so we would fall even deeper into a vicious circle of provocation and persecution which did not start with the publication of *The Satanic Verses* in September 1988. For this vicious circle can be traced back some ten centuries, to the time when devout Christians, perplexed and morally discomfited by the rapid spread of a rival faith in which Jesus was held in high esteem, discovered that if they taunted Muslims enough they could bring out their latent intolerance and violence, and thus justify plunging the sword of righteousness into their hearts.

What we are doing now – or at least what those who seek immediate publication of *The Satanic Verses* in paperback would have us do – is adding another episode to the long story of faith-baiting which has played such a large part in the conflict between Islam and Christendom. We may take comfort from the fact that the sword of Christian righteousness was long ago placed in its scabbard and is no longer likely to be used in British cities. But we should bear in mind that the new weapons of our Protestant righteousness, rifles firing rubber bullets, are already used in one British city and could be used in others. Such a development may well be improbable. But if we cannot bring ourselves to imagine it we are in danger of allowing an extremely unlikely event to become a real possibility.

We should not forget, however, that because of the undercurrent of hatred for Islam which has been developing for many years, the present situation has all the ingredients of a much greater tragedy. Even without the *Satanic Verses* affair it seems likely that a Cold War between Islam and the West would have developed in the closing decade of this century. With the Rushdie affair, this war has become in prospect even more intense.

As I write these words in the middle of April 1990, the most pressing question which remains concerns the publication of *The Satanic Verses* in paperback. In the course of the extensive media coverage given to the issue as the anniversary of the *fatwa* approached in February 1990, a number of journalists, writers, politicians and others advocated an immediate paperback edition of the book. If this advice were followed there can be little doubt, as I have argued already, that it would make matters worse. The situation we are in now is quite bad enough without embarking on a course of action which, whatever Western liberals may think of it, would seem to the Muslim community in Britain both triumphalist and contemptuous. In any case publishing *The Satanic Verses* in paperback now would really not advance the cause of freedom at all. It would only play into the hands of the minority of Muslim extremists who are hungry for further provocation and who would use a paperback edition in order to strengthen their tenuous hold on the imaginations of the vast majority of moderate Muslims in this country. In Britain, thankfully, the fuel for Muslim fundamentalism of the most cruel and extreme kind is extremely scarce. There is no good reason why we should now decide to supply it in abundance.

To say all this is not to rule out the possibility of a paperback edition of the book at some point in the rather remote future. For wounds do heal, intellectuals do sometimes learn lessons, and it is conceivable at least that there may come a time when the Muslim community itself might understand the need for a paperback edition of the book, suitably prefaced, and designed primarily for student use.

At the moment, however, the atmosphere in which such an edition could be published constructively simply does not exist. Indeed, because of the depth of anti-Islamic prejudice, such an atmosphere seems unlikely to come into being for many years. In the meantime, Penguin Books should have the good sense to continue their present policy and stay their hand on the question of a paperback edition. Only if they do so will all those who are involved in this conflict have space to negotiate and to move from the fixed positions they have adopted.

If that space is to be made use of fully, then two further moves are necessary. In the first place it would help if journalists, authors and intellectuals stopped putting pressure on the beleaguered Salman Rushdie to defend *their* principles. Salman Rushdie has already been placed in a uniquely terrible position by the Ayatollah's *fatwa*, under whose shadow he still has to live, day by day, week by week. He has quite enough to do defending his own book and his own life without being called upon to bear upon his own shoulders the entire weight of the Western liberal conscience. Yet many of Salman Rushdie's supporters, including journalists who do not know him but who are happy to editorialise in defence of his freedom to publish, have actually made his plight far more difficult by pinning him to a fixed position with their own iron principles. This kind of rigid support, motivated by ideals and principles rather than by human warmth, can only have the effect, as Dr Hesham El-Essawy observes in the open letter which I have already quoted, of driving Salman Rushdie further into 'a position of enforced martyrdom'. This is not to say that Salman Rushdie does not still need support. Because of the continuing terror of his own predicament he probably needs more support now than he has ever done before. But he needs the kind of support which will enable him to move from his fixed position in order that he may review the entire extraordinary affair not merely with his intellect, nor even with his novelist's imagination, but with the whole of that political imagination he undoubtedly possesses, but which so far he has seemed quite unable to exercise.

The second move which would greatly ease the situation is one that only the Muslim community itself can make. The Ayatollah Khomeini's *fatwa* against Salman Rushdie and his publishers was pronounced on February 14th 1989. As the anniversary approached in February 1990 this *fatwa* was renewed in Iran and it was again endorsed by a small number of extremists in this country. What these extremists should recognise, and what moderate Muslim leaders should actively seek to persuade them of, is that every time this death-threat is repeated in public, the relationship between Muslims and non-Muslims in this country suffers further damage, and it becomes more difficult for Western liberals, who are themselves pinned by history to rigid and inflexible ideals of 'freedom', to move from *their* fixed position.

The conflict has gone on long enough. As the first anniversary of the *fatwa* approached at the beginning of 1990, it seemed at times that a moment of possible reconciliation was in sight. That opportunity was missed largely because Salman Rushdie chose to offer British Muslims the rhetoric rather than the substance of reconciliation, and to hold out in his essay 'In Good Faith' an olive branch on which the leaves had already withered. That empty gesture having been made, it is time now for the real process of reconciliation to begin. Salman Rushdie himself could certainly be an important figure in this process, and he may or may not choose to co-operate with it. But we should recognise that he is not the only important figure. Just as important, and in a sense far more important, are the large numbers of writers, intellectuals and journalists who have already expressed their views on the issue, and the even larger number who have until now remained silent. It is the view which they now take, rather than Salman Rushdie's own view, which will have a decisive influence on future developments. That many will cling to the intransigent and extreme views they have already expressed seems quite clear. For history teaches us that once intellectuals have adopted extreme positions they do not easily relinquish them. What remains in doubt is whether those with more moderate views are prepared to speak loudly enough to be heard.

If they are, then the process of reconciliation can be carried forward with some degree of confidence. There can be no doubt that this process will be long, arduous, and at times frustrating. But there is no reason to suppose that it cannot be brought to completion.

Indeed it must be completed. For until it has been, and the Ayatollah Khomeini's death threat has been lifted, the life of one man in this country will continue to be in danger, and the lives of hundreds of thousands of British Muslims will continue to be lived under the shadow of an ancient religious hatred.

We should not, however, nurture the illusion that the wounds which have been opened up by the publication of a book can be healed by the writing of other books. For those wounds go deep into the hearts of whole communities and neither their nature nor their possible social and political consequences can be easily conveyed by words alone.

In this respect perhaps the last word should go to Ian Jack, the Associate Editor of *The Independent on Sunday*, a newspaper which I have frequently criticised in this book. On April 15th 1990, Ian Jack wrote an article on conditions in British prisons which deserves to be widely heeded. The article, 'Living in Filth', opened with the following paragraph:

> Of all the failures of modern Britain, perhaps the greatest is the failure of our imagination, of our ability to think ourselves into the lives of others. It might be called – though the term now seems sentimental – a rift in our common humanity.

These words, I believe, contain a profound truth which we ignore at our peril. They apply just as much to the *Satanic Verses* affair as they do to the crisis in Britain's prisons. For the great failure in both cases has been our inability to think ourselves into the lives of other people.

We need to take back our imaginative powers from the artists, novelists and poets to whom we have delegated them. For there is a danger in delegating imaginative powers just as there is a danger in delegating any powers. We need our own imaginations. For it is only when we have learnt again how to use our imagination that we can begin to repair that 'rift in our common humanity' which we have allowed to open up – both in general terms and with particular reference to the *Satanic Verses* affair.

On this last subject I have written 50,000 words but I have said nothing. Please use your imagination.

Bibliography

Commission for Racial Equality, *Law, Blasphemy and the Multi-Faith Society*, CRE, 1990;
Free Speech, CRE, 1990;
Britain: A Plural Society, CRE, 1990.
International Committee for the Defence of Salman Rushdie and his Publishers, *The Crime of Blasphemy — Why It Should Be Abolished*, 1989.

*

Ahmad, Hazrat Mirza Tahir, *Murder in the Name of Allah*, Lutterworth, 1989.
Akhtar, Shabbir, *Be Careful with Muhammad! The Salman Rushdie Affair*, Bellew, 1989.
Appignanesi, Lisa, and Maitland, Sara, *The Rushdie File*, Fourth Estate, 1989.
Armstrong, Karen, *Holy War: The Crusades and their Impact on Today's World*, Macmillan, 1988.
Bettelheim, Bruno, *Recollections and Reflections*, Thames and Hudson, 1990.
Cohn, Norman, *The Pursuit of the Millennium: Revolutionary Millennarians and Mystical Anarchists of the Middle Ages*, Paladin 1970;
Warrant for Genocide: the Myth of the Jewish World Conspiracy and the Protocols of the Elders of Zion, Penguin, 1970;
Europe's Inner Demons, Paladin, 1976.
Gager, John G., *The Origins of Anti-Semitism*, Oxford University Press, 1985.
Greer, Germaine, *The Female Eunuch*, Paladin, 1971.
Hill, Christopher, *The World Turned Upside Down*, Penguin, 1975.
Jussawalla, Feroza, 'Resurrecting the Prophet: the Case of Salman the Otherwise', *Public Culture*, Vol. 2, No. 1, Fall, 1989.
Kabbani, Rana, *Letter to Christendom*, Virago, 1989;
Europe's Myths of Orient, Pandora, 1988.
Lee, Simon, 'First Introductory Paper' in *Law, Blasphemy and the Multi-Faith Society*, Commission for Racial Equality, 1990.
Mazrui, Ali M., 'The Satanic Verses or a Satanic Novel? Moral Dilemmas of the Rushdie Affair', in *Free Speech*, Commission for Racial Equality, 1990.
Parekh, Bhikhu, 'The Rushdie Affair and the British Press', in *Free Speech*, Commission for Racial Equality, 1990.

Parkes, James, *The Conflict of the Church and the Synagogue: A Study in the Origins of Antisemitism*, London, 1934;
Antisemitism, Valentine Mitchell, London 1963.

Poliakov, Léon, *The History of Anti-Semitism* Vol 1-3, Routledge and Kegan Paul, 1974.

Poulter, Sebastian, 'Cultural Pluralism and its Limits' in *Britain: A Plural Society*, Commission for Racial Equality, 1990.

Qureshi, Shoaib, and Khan, Javed, *The Politics of Satanic Verses*, Muslim Community Studies Institute, 1989.

Raleigh, V. Soni, et al, 'Suicides Among Immigrants from the Indian Subcontinent', *British Journal of Psychiatry* (1990), 156, pp 46-50.

Ruthven, Malise, *A Satanic Affair: Salman Rushdie and the Rage of Islam*, Chatto, 1990.

Scribner, R. W., *For the Sake of Simple Folk: Popular Propaganda for the German Reformation*, Cambridge University Press, 1981.

Shachar, Isaiah, *The Judensau: A Medieval Anti-Jewish Motif and its History*, Warburg Institute, 1974.

Soyinka, Wole, 'Jihad for Freedom', *Index on Censorship* 18.5, May/June 1989.

Tawney, R. H., *Religion and the Rise of Capitalism*, Penguin, 1938.

Trachtenberg, Joshua, *The Devil and the Jews*, Newhaven, 1943.

Walter, Nicolas, *Blasphemy Ancient and Modern*, Rationalist Press Association, 1990.

Weldon, Fay, *Sacred Cows*, Chatto, 1989.

Note

As this book went to press, Tariq Modood's excellent article, 'British Asian Muslims and the Rushdie Affair', was published in *The Political Quarterly* (Vol 61, no 2, April 1990, pp 143-160). The article deals with many aspects of the affair not covered in this book and deserves a wide readership. At the same time Asaf Hussain's short historical study, *Western Conflict with Islam: Survey of the Anti-Islamic Tradition*, was published by Volcano Books. I have unfortunately been unable to consult it.